TECHNICAL REPORT

Developing a Defense Sector Assessment Rating Tool

Agnes Gereben Schaefer, Lynn E. Davis,
Ely Ratner, Molly Dunigan, Jeremiah Goulka,
Heather Peterson, K. Jack Riley

Prepared for the Office of the Secretary of Defense

NATIONAL DEFENSE RESEARCH INSTITUTE

The research described in this report was prepared for the Office of the Secretary of Defense (OSD). The research was conducted in the RAND National Defense Research Institute, a federally funded research and development center sponsored by OSD, the Joint Staff, the Unified Combatant Commands, the Navy, the Marine Corps, the defense agencies, and the defense Intelligence Community under Contract W74V8H-06-C-0002.

Library of Congress Control Number: 2010935903

ISBN: 978-0-8330-5030-4

The RAND Corporation is a nonprofit institution that helps improve policy and decisionmaking through research and analysis. RAND's publications do not necessarily reflect the opinions of its research clients and sponsors.

RAND® is a registered trademark.

Published 2010 by the RAND Corporation
1776 Main Street, P.O. Box 2138, Santa Monica, CA 90407-2138
1200 South Hayes Street, Arlington, VA 22202-5050
4570 Fifth Avenue, Suite 600, Pittsburgh, PA 15213-2665
RAND URL: http://www.rand.org/
To order RAND documents or to obtain additional information, contact
Distribution Services: Telephone: (310) 451-7002;
Fax: (310) 451-6915; Email: order@rand.org

Preface

This report presents the conceptual framework and methodology used to develop the Defense Sector Assessment Rating Tool (DSART). The DSART is designed to assess the state of the defense sector in a given country, and, in turn, can be used as a basis for prioritizing and allocating security assistance resources, as well as evaluating the progress of defense sector reform over time. The DSART itself can be found at the end of this report.

This report should be of interest to policymakers and others concerned with the planning, management, and implementation of defense sector reform activities and programs. Readers may also find the following RAND publications to be of interest:

- *A Framework to Assess Programs for Building Partnerships,* by Jennifer D. P. Moroney, Jefferson P. Marquis, Cathryn Quantic Thurston, and Gregory F. Treverton (MG-863-OSD).
- *Making Liberia Safe: Transformation of the National Security Sector,* by David C. Gompert, Olga Oliker, Brooke Stearns Lawson, Keith Crane, and K. Jack Riley (MG-529-OSD).
- *Clean, Lean and Able: A Strategy for Defense Development,* by David C. Gompert, Olga Oliker, and Anga R. Timilsina (OP-101-RC).

This research was sponsored by the Office of the Secretary of Defense and the Defense Security Cooperation Agency and conducted within the International Security and Defense Policy Center of the RAND National Defense Research Institute, a federally funded research and development center sponsored by the Office of the Secretary of Defense, the Joint Staff, the Unified Combatant Commands, the Navy, the Marine Corps, the defense agencies, and the defense Intelligence Community.

For more information on RAND's International Security and Defense Policy Center, contact the Director, James Dobbins. He can be reached by email at James_Dobbins@rand. org; by phone at 703-413-1100, extension 5134; or by mail at the RAND Corporation, 1200 South Hayes Street, Arlington, VA 22202.

Questions or comments are welcome and may be directed to the project co-leaders:

Agnes Gereben Schaefer
RAND Corporation
4570 Fifth Avenue, Suite 600
Pittsburgh, PA 15213
(412) 683-2300 x4488
Agnes_Schaefer@rand.org

Lynn E. Davis
RAND Corporation
1200 South Hayes Street
Arlington, VA 22202
(703) 413-1100 x5399
Lynn_Davis@rand.org

More information about RAND is available at www.rand.org.

Contents

Figure and Tables

Figure

Tables

Summary

The U.S. government spends billions of dollars annually on foreign assistance. Foreign assistance programs span many agencies, including the U.S. Department of State (DoS), the U.S. Agency for International Development (USAID), and the U.S. Department of Defense (DoD). There is currently a variety of assessment tools and frameworks to assist in the design of foreign assistance programs and allocation of resources.[1] However, there is no comprehensive tool to assist policymakers in assessing the state of the defense sector in a given country, to provide them with a systematic way of determining a country's capabilities to achieve various security goals that the U.S. government may have, or to monitor the success of defense sector programs over time. This study aimed to fill that gap and design the Defense Sector Assessment Rating Tool (DSART). The DSART can be found at the end of this report.

For the purpose of the DSART, the defense sector is defined as the uniformed military, plus the military and civilian management, accountability, and oversight systems, mechanisms, and processes that sustain it.

U.S. Goals For Defense Sector Reform

The United States could have a variety of goals for defense sector reform in a given country. One goal could be to support the country in its efforts to better manage its own security problems and potentially partner with the United States and other countries in international military operations. Such reforms would involve the country changing its defense institutions and processes to include those capacities that the United States views as critical for effective military planning and operations (e.g., civilian control of the military, military professionalism).

Another set of goals could be to improve the country's ability to counter specific threats and improve its own internal security and thereby contribute to U.S. security. These threats could include terrorism and insurgency, drug trafficking, porous land or sea borders, piracy, and instability in the aftermath of a conflict. Foreign assistance that seeks to promote this set of U.S. goals could involve improving a country's military capabilities for surveillance and interdiction, training its military in counternarcotics or counterterrorism operations, and helping establish processes for military coordination with civilian law-enforcement organizations. The structure of the DSART flows directly from these potential goals for defense sector reform.

---

[1] See the appendix for a list of assessment tools.

Structure of DSART

The first section of the DSART sets the stage for the subsequent assessments, and the assessor is asked to answer questions about the characteristics of the defense sector in a country. The focus areas and questions were drawn from the many assessment tools that are used by the U.S. government, foreign governments, international organizations, and nongovernmental organizations (NGOs) to assess countries' security or defense sectors.

The introductory section is followed by six assessments, the first of which focuses on the country's defense institutions and processes and how they match up with a set of capacities that the United States views as "critical" in any defense sector. These capacities are defined in various U.S. government documents. The DSART assessor is asked to provide a qualitative appraisal and then a quantitative score of the country's "critical" capacities on a scale of 1 (entirely lacking) to 5 (strong and no major improvement needed). Once the deficiencies in capacities have been identified, the section ends by asking a series of questions about the prospects for reforming those areas in which deficiencies were found. The end result is an assessment that identifies deficiencies in the country's defense institutions and processes, as well as an assessment of the prospects for reform in the deficient areas.

The subsequent sections in the DSART assess the country's capabilities to carry out operations to counter high-priority internal security threats (terrorism and insurgency, drug trafficking, porous land or sea borders, piracy, and instability in the aftermath of a conflict). The research team drew from U.S. government planning documents, historical case studies, and discussions with subject-matter experts to identify a list of "critical functions" necessary to respond to each of these security threats.

In these sections, the assessor is asked to provide a qualitative appraisal and then a quantitative score of the country's capabilities to carry out these "critical" functions on a scale of 1 (entirely lacking) to 5 (strong and no major improvement needed). Once the deficiencies in capabilities have been identified, the sections end by asking a series of questions about the prospects for reforming those areas in which deficiencies were found. The end results identify deficiencies in the country's capability to conduct counterterrorism and counterinsurgency, counternarcotics, border and maritime security, counterpiracy, or postconflict stabilization operations and provide an assessment of the prospects for reform in the deficient areas.

The Way Ahead

The DSART can play a vital role in assisting U.S. policymakers in identifying deficiencies in a country's defense sector and then prioritizing and allocating foreign assistance resources. Once U.S. policymakers decide that a country's defense sector will need to be assessed, a decision will also need to be made about which assessment tools are most appropriate for their goals. For instance, the DSART could be used by itself or in combination with other assessment tools, such as the Criminal Justice Sector Assessment Rating Tool, depending on what issues policymakers are most interested in understanding. Once it is decided that the DSART should be used to assess a country's defense sector, the assessor always fills out Section One of the DSART, "Characteristics of the Defense Sector." The assessor then completes those assessments that are applicable to the chosen goals. In some cases, only one of these assessments may be applicable to the country; in other cases, multiple assessments may need to be completed because the United States has multiple goals. The completed DSART assessment is then returned to U.S. policymakers, who review it and use it as background for deciding whether to undertake defense sector reforms and how resources should be allocated for those reforms. The initial DSART assessment of a country's defense sector should be viewed as only the starting point for what will need to be a series of activities, potentially over many years, that will involve programs and follow-on assessments.

The DSART, in its structured set of questions and assessments of critical defense sector capacities and the capabilities needed to meet different types of internal security threats, is similar to the assessment tools of other U.S. government agencies and multinational organizations. The DSART does, however, lend itself to being used for a more formal and systematic assessment of these capacities and capabilities. To this end, the assessor could take additional steps to validate the information that is collected, e.g., answering the questions in the DSART through structured interviews, holding workshops with a cross-section of local experts, or conducting tabletop exercises for the qualitative evaluations.

The DSART could be used by countries other than the United States to assess either their own defense sector capabilities or those of countries to which they are providing assistance. The DSART could also be used by multilateral organizations to assess the countries to which they are or may wish to provide assistance.

While the DSART is now ready for use, U.S. goals for defense sector reform may evolve. The DSART is designed with a flexible architecture so that it can be adapted to a changing security environment. Our goal is that the tool will continue to evolve as it is used in different countries and with different goals in mind.

Acknowledgments

We are grateful for the support and guidance we received from our sponsors at the Office of the Secretary of Defense and the Defense Security Cooperation Agency. In particular, we would like to thank our project monitors, Colonel Gregory Hermsmeyer and Alden Sanborn. We also thank those who provided input during the research process, including Julie Werbel, Christina Rosati, James Walsh, Steve Peterson, Cara Abercrombie, and Constantine Xefeteris. We benefited from valuable interagency feedback on interim versions of the DSART from representatives from DoD, U.S. European Command, U.S. Africa Command, USAID, DoS, the Executive Office of U.S. Attorneys, the Warsaw Initiative Fund, and OPNAV N52, the U.S. Navy's Directorate for International Engagement. We are particularly grateful to Michelle Hughes and Thomas Pope for their assistance in field-testing the DSART on two occasions and for their feedback on the DSART's utility during those field tests.

We also thank our RAND colleagues, including James Dobbins and Michael Lostumbo for their reviews of interim briefings and drafts, and Stuart Johnson, Jennifer D. P. Moroney, Jefferson P. Marquis, and Terrence K. Kelly for their feedback and input into the DSART. This report benefited greatly from the helpful comments and suggested revisions proposed by our reviewers. Finally, we thank Lauren Skrabala, Jocelyn Lofstrom, and Michelle McMullen for their assistance in preparing the final document.

The content and conclusions in this report are solely the responsibility of the authors.

Abbreviations

ATRAT	Afghan Training Readiness Assessment Tool
CJSART	Criminal Justice Sector Assessment Rating Tool
DAC	Development Assistance Committee
DIB	Defense Institution Building
DoD	U.S. Department of Defense
DoS	U.S. Department of State
DSART	Defense Sector Assessment Rating Tool
GDP	gross domestic product
ICAF	Interagency Conflict Assessment Framework
ISAF	International Security Assistance Force
MoD	ministry of defense
NATO	North Atlantic Treaty Organization
NGO	nongovernmental organization
OECD	Organisation for Economic Co-Operation and Development
OSD	Office of the Secretary of Defense
PfP	Partnership for Peace
SSR	security sector reform
USAID	U.S. Agency for International Development
WIF	Warsaw Initiative Fund

CHAPTER ONE

Introduction

Need for This Study

The U.S. government spends billions of dollars annually on foreign assistance, and foreign assistance programs span many agencies, including the U.S. Department of State (DoS), the U.S. Agency for International Development (USAID), and the U.S. Department of Defense (DoD).[1] There is currently a variety of assessment tools and frameworks to assist in the design of foreign assistance programs and allocation of resources. For instance, the Organisation for Economic Co-Operation and Development (OECD) Development Assistance Committee's (DAC's) *Handbook on Security System Reform: Supporting Security and Justice* presents general questions that could be used by countries and multilateral organizations to assess the security sector in a country and the need for reform.[2] In addition, DoS has developed the Criminal Justice Sector Assessment Rating Tool (CJSART), which can be used to assess "whether [a country's] criminal justice sector has the adequate laws, judicial and prosecutorial professionals, effective policing, penal structure, and international commitment to ultimately provide equal access to justice and security for its citizens."[3]

However, there is no comprehensive tool to assist policymakers in assessing the state of the defense sector in a given country, to provide them with a systematic way of determining a country's ability to achieve various security goals that the U.S. government may have, or to monitor the success of defense sector reform programs over time.

This study addresses that gap by designing the Defense Sector Assessment Rating Tool (DSART). The DSART can be found at the end of this report. For the purposes of the DSART, the defense sector is defined as the uniformed military, plus the military and civilian management, accountability, and oversight systems, mechanisms, and processes that sustain it. The DSART is designed to assess any country across the spectrum of defense sector development—from countries that have weak or underdeveloped defense sectors to those, like Warsaw Initiative Fund (WIF)/Partnership for Peace (PfP) countries, that have relatively mature defense sectors.

---

[1] For the goals and programs, see U.S. Department of Defense, *Fiscal Year 2010 Budget Request, Summary Justification*, May 2009, p. 1-13.

[2] Organisation for Economic Co-Operation and Development, *OECD DAC Handbook on Security System Reform: Supporting Security and Justice*, Paris, 2007.

[3] U.S. Department of State, Bureau for International Narcotics and Law Enforcement Affairs, *Criminal Justice Sector Assessment Rating Tool: A U.S. Government Interagency Framework to Assess the Capacity of International Criminal Justice Systems*, 2008, p. 4.

The U.S. Foreign Assistance Framework and Security Sector Reform

The Foreign Assistance Act of 1961 (Pub. L. 87-195) reorganized U.S. foreign assistance programs, separated military and nonmilitary aid, and established USAID. The foreign assistance framework was later established to align foreign aid with U.S. government priorities and is built around five foreign policy objectives:[4]

- peace and security, including preventing, mitigating, and recovering from internal or external conflict
- governing justly and democratically, including making governments accountable to their people by controlling corruption, protecting civil rights, and strengthening the rule of law
- investing in people, including appropriate expenditures on health and education
- economic growth, including reducing barriers to entry for businesses, establishing a suitable trade policy, and promoting fiscal accountability
- humanitarian assistance, including emergency relief and rehabilitation.

Over the past few years, security sector reform (SSR) efforts have become an increasingly important aspect of foreign assistance. According to USAID, DoD, and DoS, SSR is defined as

> the set of policies, plans, programs, and activities that a government undertakes to improve the way it provides safety, security, and justice. The overall objective is to provide these services in a way that promotes an effective and legitimate public service that is transparent, accountable to civilian authority, and responsive to the needs of the public. From a donor perspective, SSR is an umbrella term that might include integrated activities in support of: defense and armed forces reform; civilian management and oversight; justice; police; corrections; intelligence reform; national security planning and strategy support; border management; disarmament, demobilization and reintegration (DDR); and/or reduction of armed violence.[5]

The U.S. foreign assistance framework identifies SSR and security sector governance as key program areas in support of the following foreign policy objectives: (1) peace and security and (2) just and democratic governance.[6]

The security sector comprises various actors, including state security providers (e.g., military forces, civilian police, intelligence services, coast guards, border guards), governmental security management and oversight bodies (e.g., the president; prime minister; ministries of defense, public administration, interior, justice, and foreign affairs; the judiciary; financial management bodies), civil society (e.g., think tanks, universities, advocacy organizations), and nonstate providers of justice and security.[7] The security sector also includes several subsectors, such as defense, criminal justice, law-enforcement reform and restructuring, and community security initiatives. DoD's primary role in SSR is supporting the reform, restructuring, or re-

---

[4] See U.S. Department of State, "Foreign Assistance Standardized Program Structure and Definitions," January 2010.

[5] U.S. Agency for International Development, U.S. Department of Defense, and U.S. Department of State, *Security Sector Reform*, Washington, D.C., 2009, p. 3.

[6] See U.S. Department of State, 2010.

[7] U.S. Agency for International Development, U.S. Department of Defense, and U.S. Department of State, 2009, pp. 3–4.

establishment of the armed forces and the defense sector across the operational spectrum.[8] The goals for this include the following:[9]

- Promote democratic control over armed forces through a legal and constitutional framework and civilian management.
- Delineate clear roles and responsibilities for internal security between the military and police.
- Review security threats and develop the capacity to respond to them.
- Increase transparency and oversight of military expenditures.
- Develop representative armed forces.
- Balance "train-and-equip" efforts with governance and institutional and human capacity building.

The DSART is designed to assist DoD as it seeks to accomplish these goals. The DSART is also designed to take into account possible intersections between the defense sector and other sectors, such as integrated border management or intelligence reform.

Structure of the DSART

The United States has a variety of goals for defense sector reform in a given country. One goal could be to support the country in its efforts to better manage its security problems and potentially to partner with the United States and other countries in international military operations. Such reforms would involve the country changing its defense institutions and processes to include those capacities that the United States views as critical for effective military planning and operations (e.g., civilian control of the military, military professionalism).

Another set of goals could be to improve the country's ability to counter specific threats and improve its own internal security, as well as potentially improve U.S. security. These threats could include terrorism and insurgency, drug trafficking, porous land or sea borders, piracy, and instability in the aftermath of a conflict. Foreign assistance that seeks to promote this set of U.S. goals could involve improving a country's military capabilities for surveillance and interdiction, training its military in counternarcotics or counterterrorism operations, and helping establish processes for military coordination with civilian law-enforcement organizations. The structure of the DSART flows directly from these potential goals.

Supporting U.S. partners in defending their national territory is another potential security goal of the United States, but this goal is not included in the DSART. This is the case because such an assessment would require an understanding not only of the military capabilities of a partner but also those of the enemy and, potentially, the United States as well, if the United States were to plan on being involved.

The first section of the DSART examines the characteristics of the defense sector in the country being assessed. Section One begins with a set of open-ended questions about

---

[8] U.S. Agency for International Development, U.S. Department of Defense, and U.S. Department of State, 2009, p. 3.

[9] See Eden Cole, Kerstin Eppert, and Katrin Kinzelbach, eds., *Public Oversight of the Security Sector: A Handbook for Civil Society Organizations*, Geneva: Geneva Centre for the Democratic Control of Armed Forces, 2008; also see COL Gregory Hermsmeyer, "Security Sector Reform: DoD Guidance, Organization and Authorities," briefing, undated.

the military forces in the country (e.g., their role, composition, and capabilities) and then focuses on the various institutions and processes that sustain and exercise control over them (e.g., the ministry of defense, strategy, planning, and budgeting processes). The section ends with a set of open-ended questions aimed at determining the country's overall political, economic, and security environment. This section provides the background and context for the subsequent assessment sections of the tool.

The introductory section of the DSART is followed by six assessments. The first assesses a country's defense institutions and processes and how they match up with a set of capacities that the United States views as "critical" in any defense sector. The other five assessments focus on the country's capability to respond to high-priority internal security threats: terrorism and insurgency, drug trafficking, porous land or sea borders, piracy, and instability in the aftermath of a conflict, respectively.

Organization of This Report

This report is organized into three chapters and an appendix. Chapter Two describes how the DSART was developed based on current assessment tools that are used by the U.S. government, international organizations, and nongovernmental organizations (NGOs) as well as our own research. Chapter Three describes how to use the DSART now and how it can be adapted to changes in the future. The appendix contains a compilation of the assessment tools that we examined in the course of developing the DSART. The DSART can be found at the end of this report.

CHAPTER TWO

Development of the DSART

This chapter describes how the DSART was developed and the analytical and research basis for the questions and assessment categories. In the process of developing the DSART, drafts were circulated widely for comments and suggestions from U.S. government agencies. In addition, two assessment teams tested the DSART in the field and shared their reactions and recommendations. All of these were incorporated into this version of the DSART.

Section One: Characteristics of the Defense Sector

This section of the DSART asks questions about the characteristics of the defense sector in a given country and sets the stage for the assessment sections of the tool. What the assessor is seeking through these questions is a general understanding of the defense sector in the country and enough information to be able to conduct the assessments that follow.

The questions in this section were drawn primarily from the many assessment tools that are used by the U.S. government, foreign governments, international organizations, and NGOs to assess countries' security or defense sectors. See the appendix for a complete compilation of the assessment tools that we examined.

The OECD issued its policy guidance *Security System Reform and Governance* in 2005. It covers three interrelated challenges faced by all states: (1) developing a clear institutional framework for the provision of security that integrates security and development policy and includes all relevant actors, (2) strengthening the governance of the security institutions, and (3) building capable and professional security forces that are accountable to civil authorities.[1] The 2007 *OECD DAC Handbook on Security System Reform* was developed to provide guidance to operationalize these guidelines and close the gap between policy and practice. Because the *OECD DAC Handbook* was developed through broad agreement among OECD states and is accepted among OECD states as the guidepost for SSR, it served as the foundation for our development of the categories and questions in Section One.

In the section "Undertaking Security System Reform Assessments," the *OECD DAC Handbook* outlines three analytical categories that should be included in any SSR assessment: (1) political economy and conflict analysis, (2) governance and capacity of security and justice institutions, (3) other frameworks and programs.[2] Table 2.1 outlines the types

---

[1] Organisation for Economic Co-Operation and Development, *Security Sector Reform and Governance*, Paris, 2005, p. 16.

[2] OECD, 2007, pp. 50–52.

Table 2.1
Illustrative OECD DAC SSR Assessment

Analytical Category	Key Elements	Illustrative Questions
Political economy and conflict analysis	Type of state: postconflict, fragile, transitional political system corruption in government and security system economic system, resources	What type of state is it? What type of political system? Are essential public services being delivered? To whom? Is there separation of powers between the legislature, executive, and judiciary? How does corruption affect the government?
	Political will/drivers of change: systems/institutions/ actors/ processes enabling change factors underlying resistance to change	What are the policy trends? What is the role of power structures and relations? What are the incentives and disincentives for these different actors to support reform?
Governance and capacity of security and justice institutions	State institutions and actors: executive legislative municipal government security and justice providers (roles, mandates, functions)	Which state institutions have a role in security and justice provision? How many uniformed forces exist, and is there a hierarchy among them? Are the same security forces responsible for internal and external security?
	Nonstate institutions and actors: Other actors involved in security	What nonstate security and justice actors are there? What are their respective roles, missions, and functions? How legitimate are they? What is their relationship to the formal security system? What gaps do they fill and how?
Other programs	Political programs and initiatives	What political programs is the government involved in that could provide an entry point to SSR? What initiatives are donors supporting to strengthen governance?
	International assistance programs	Are there existing areas of international support that could provide an entry point to engaging in SSR? Are any international actors already providing support for SSR? If so, is it provided by development agencies, embassies, or security agencies?

of questions that are included under these three analytical categories.[3] We have incorporated each of these analytical categories into the DSART and included many of these same questions.

In the section "Defense Reform," the *OECD DAC Handbook* identifies six major areas that should be addressed in any defense sector assessment. We have incorporated these areas into the DSART, along with many of the questions (see Table 2.2).[4]

---

[3]   OECD, 2007, pp. 52–56.

[4]   OECD, 2007, pp. 126–127. These points follow from the key issues that should be identified in any assessment of defense reform: developing democratic control over defense policy and the armed forces, including a constitutional and legal framework and civilian oversight and management; strengthening the process for reviewing security threats and developing the capacity to respond to them; delineating clear roles and responsibilities with the police for internal security; introducing integrated approaches to policy development, military expenditure, human resource planning, and management of military assets; encouraging civil society debate and citizens' awareness of and engagement with defense reform issues; promoting reform in training and the career development of military personnel, and career transition and resettlement plans for those

Table 2.2
Illustrative OECD DAC Defense Sector Assessment

Major Areas to Address	Questions to Ask
Context	How does the military's history inform public and military perceptions of the role of the military in society?
	How politicized is the military, in its leadership as well as among rank and file?
	What are judged to be the main strengths and weaknesses of the military, by civilians, politicians, defense experts, NGOs, and the military itself?
Accountability and oversight	What is the chain of command and division of responsibilities?
	What oversight mechanisms, internal and external to the defense sector, exist for military budgets and expenditures?
	How transparent are military policy, spending, and management to parliamentarians, the media, and the general public?
Capacity	Are force design, deployment, personnel structure, and training compatible with the internal and external threat environment from a military perspective?
	Is the military engaged in international peacekeeping operations, and which (positive and negative) effects does this have on the military overall?
Management	How are policy development, programming, planning, and management organized?
	What are the roles of political and military bodies?
	How are budgets prepared and implemented?
	Is there a planning cycle, and how are responsibilities divided?
Coordination with other parts of the security sector	What is the role of the military in internal security, and how is it distinguished from that of the police and from paramilitary forces?
	What are the rules and procedures for triggering a military response to an internal security crisis?
	What is the role of the military in border control?
Engagement of the international community	How, if at all, are international actors involved in defense reform efforts?
	Are they guided by a comprehensive approach to defense reform? How important is the promotion of governance in these efforts?

In addition to the *OECD DAC Handbook*, we drew on the following tools in the development of the DSART:[5]

- USAID's SSR Assessment Framework, particularly its emphasis on the importance of local context, institutions, and stakeholders.[6]
- The DoS Office of Reconstruction and Development's *Interagency Conflict Assessment Framework* (ICAF), particularly the four steps of the ICAF conflict diagnosis.[7]

---

leaving the armed forces; promoting ethnic and social balance and equal opportunity policies in the defense sector; and strengthening regional arrangements for military cooperation, confidence building, arms control, and disarmament.

[5]   For a more detailed description of these tools, see the appendix.

[6]   This tool is still in development. See U.S. Agency for International Development, "USG SSR Assessment Framework," February 2, 2009.

[7]   U.S. Department of State, Office of the Coordinator for Reconstruction and Development, *Interagency Conflict Assessment Framework*, Washington, D.C., 2008.

- The DoS Bureau for International Narcotics and Law Enforcement Affairs *Criminal Justice System Assessment Rating Tool,* for its systematic description of the judicial processes.[8]
- DoD's Defense Institution Building (DIB) Assessment Methodology, for its questions related to professional military education and logistics.[9]
- Assessment tools that DoD and NATO developed for use in assessing security forces in Iraq and Afghanistan, for their questions related to military readiness.[10]

Section Two: Assessment of Defense Institutions and Processes

The DSART has six assessments linked to potential U.S. goals. The first assessment focuses on a country's defense institutions and processes and how they match up with a set of capacities that the United States views as "critical" in any defense sector. The critical capacities in the DSART are those defined in various U.S. government documents:

- civilian control of the military in practice, not just organization[11]
- systems of defense planning, procurement, budgeting, and financial management, including contracting and auditing[12]
- professionalism of military forces in terms of education and training[13]
- military personnel policies capable of recruiting, training, and retaining high-quality soldiers and officers who are representative of society as a whole[14]
- effective military command-and-control and logistics organizations[15]
- incorporation of rule of law and human rights components into military and ministry of defense training programs[16]
- security forces that carry out their functions in accordance with the principles of accountability, transparency, public participation, and respect for human rights.[17]

---

[8] U.S. Department of State, Bureau for International Narcotics and Law Enforcement Affairs, 2008.

[9] See U.S. Department of Defense, "Warsaw Initiative Fund Defense Institution Building Assessment Methodology," undated(c).

[10] In particular, see the Afghan Training Readiness Assessment Tool (ATRAT). For an overview of this tool, see "Measuring ANSF Capabilities Through Milestones," *The Enduring Ledger* (Combined Security Transition Command–Afghanistan), April 2009, p. 18.

[11] See *Partnership for Peace: Framework Document Issued by the Heads of State and Government Participating in the Meeting of the North Atlantic Council,* Brussels, January 10, 1994; Foreign Assistance Act of 1961 (Pub. L. 87-195), Chapter 5, Section 541; U.S. Agency for International Development, U.S. Department of Defense, and U.S. Department of State, 2009, p. 7.

[12] See *Partnership for Peace,* 1994; "Defense Institution Reform Initiative (DIRI) Priorities" in Defense Security Cooperation Agency, *Fiscal Year 2011 Budget Estimates,* Washington, D.C., February 2010.

[13] Foreign Assistance Act of 1961 (Pub. L. 87-195), Chapter 5, "International Military Education and Training."

[14] See "Defense Institution Reform Initiative (DIRI) Priorities" in Defense Security Cooperation Agency, 2010.

[15] See "Defense Institution Reform Initiative (DIRI) Priorities" in Defense Security Cooperation Agency, 2010.

[16] See *Partnership for Peace,* 1994, and U.S. Agency for International Development, U.S. Department of Defense, and U.S. Department of State, 2009, p. 4.

[17] See *Partnership for Peace,* 1994, and U.S. Agency for International Development, U.S. Department of Defense, and U.S. Department of State, 2009, p. 5.

The information required for this assessment is collected in Section One of the DSART, through answers to the questions about the characteristics of the defense sector. While these "critical" capacities are interrelated, the DSART does not prioritize them, as this has not been done in U.S. defense reform strategies or documents. The assessor evaluates a country's capacities individually.

The assessor using the DSART is then asked to provide a qualitative appraisal and a quantitative scoring of the country's capacities on a scale of 1 (entirely lacking) to 5 (strong and no major improvement needed). Once the assessor has discovered where deficiencies exist, Section Two ends by asking a series of questions regarding the country's prospects for reforming those areas in which deficiencies were found. The end result is an assessment that identifies deficiencies in the country's defense institutions and processes, as well as an assessment of the prospects for reform in the deficient areas.

Sections Three Through Seven: Assessments of Capabilities to Counter Security Threats

Beyond the goal of reforming the institutions and processes of a country's defense sector, the United States could seek to help a country respond to high-priority internal security threats, such as terrorism and insurgency, drug trafficking, porous land or sea borders, piracy, and instability in the aftermath of a conflict.

Drawing on U.S. government planning documents, historical case studies, and discussions with subject-matter experts, we identified a list of "critical" functions needed to respond to each of these internal security threats.

These sections begin with additional questions as background for conducting the assessments. In each of these assessments, the assessor is asked to provide a qualitative appraisal and then a quantitative score of the country's capabilities to carry out the "critical" functions on a scale of 1 (entirely lacking) to 5 (strong and no major improvement needed). Once the deficiencies in capabilities have been identified, each section ends by asking a series of questions regarding the prospects for reforming the areas in which deficiencies were found. The end results identify deficiencies in the country's capabilities to conduct counterterrorism and counterinsurgency, counternarcotics, border and maritime security, counterpiracy, and postconflict stabilization operations and provide an assessment of the prospects for reform in the deficient areas.

Section Three: Counterterrorism and Counterinsurgency

Assisting other countries in improving their counterterrorism and counterinsurgency capabilities is one potential U.S. security goal. The threat in a country could come from insurgents, from terrorists, or, in some cases, from both.

Although insurgent and terrorist groups often have different goals and employ different tactics, the DSART does not define counterterrorism and counterinsurgency as separate security threats for the purposes of an assessment.[18] After a careful review of the critical functions

---

[18] Debates are ongoing as to the similarities and differences between terrorist and insurgent groups. See U.S. Central Intelligence Agency, "Guide to the Analysis of Insurgency," Washington, D.C., January 5, 2009, p. 2; Daniel L. Byman, "Friends Like These: Counterinsurgency and the War on Terrorism," *International Security*, Vol. 31, No. 2, Fall 2006, pp. 84, 86; David J. Kilcullen, "Countering Global Insurgency," *Journal of Strategic Studies*, Vol. 28, No. 4, August 2005, pp. 603–605.

for counterterrorism and counterinsurgency, we found that these functions were actually very similar.

Given the recent conflicts in Iraq and Afghanistan, there is an expanding body of information on the capabilities needed to respond to terrorist and insurgent groups. The U.S. government has also developed manuals for counterinsurgency operations. We drew on these sources as well as "lessons-learned" reports from the Center for Army Lessons Learned, the U.S. Army War College, and the RAND Corporation.

We identified the following "critical" functions needed for counterterrorism and counterinsurgency operations:

- Maintain security throughout the country.[19]
- Collect and analyze intelligence.[20]
- Provide policing and law enforcement.[21]
- Protect critical infrastructure.[22]
- Carry out military surveillance and interdiction.[23]
- Integrate strategic communication.[24]
- Hold territory and control roadways, waterways, and airspace.[25]
- Contribute to the design and delivery of an integrated government strategy and operations.[26]
- Train military forces for counterterrorism or counterinsurgency operations.[27]
- Control corruption.[28]
- Disrupt financing by terrorist or insurgent groups from within or outside the country.[29]
- Deny support to terrorist or insurgent groups from domestic populations or from outside the country.[30]

---

[19] See David C. Gompert, John Gordon IV, Adam Grissom, David R. Frelinger, Seth G. Jones, Martin C. Libicki, Edward O'Connell, Brooke Stearns Lawson, and Robert E. Hunter, *War by Other Means—Building Complete and Balanced Capabilities for Counterinsurgency: RAND Counterinsurgency Study—Final Report*, Santa Monica, Calif.: RAND Corporation, MG-595/2-OSD, 2008. See also Agnes Gereben Schaefer, Benjamin Bahney, and K. Jack Riley, *Security in Mexico: Implications for U.S. Policy Options*, Santa Monica, Calif.: RAND Corporation, MG-876-RC, 2009.

[20] Headquarters, U.S. Department of the Army, *Counterinsurgency*, Field Manual 3-24, Washington, D.C., December 16, 2006, p. 3-24; Gompert, Gordon, et al., 2008.

[21] See Jason Beers, *Community Oriented Policing and Counterinsurgency: A Conceptual Model*, thesis, Ft. Leavenworth, Kan.: U.S. Army Command and Staff College, 2007; and James Corum, *Training Indigenous Forces for Counterinsurgency: A Tale of Two Insurgencies*, Carlisle, Pa.: Strategic Studies Institute, U.S. Army War College, March 2006.

[22] Headquarters, U.S. Department of the Army, 2006, p. 5-14, 2009a, p. 3-7.

[23] Headquarters, U.S. Department of the Army, 2006, p. 3-26.

[24] See David P. Anders, *Developing an Operational Level Strategic Communication Model for Counterinsurgency*, Carlisle, Pa.: Center for Strategic Leadership, U.S. Army War College, February 24, 2009.

[25] Headquarters, U.S. Department of the Army, 2006, p. 5-19.

[26] See David C. Gompert, Terrence K. Kelly, Brooke Stearns Lawson, Michelle Parker, and Kimberly Colloton, *Reconstruction Under Fire: Unifying Civil and Military Counterinsurgency*, Santa Monica, Calif.: RAND Corporation, MG-870-OSD, 2009.

[27] Headquarters, U.S. Department of the Army, 2006, p. 6-61.

[28] See Schaefer, Bahney, and Riley, 2009.

[29] Kilcullen, 2005, p. 607.

[30] Kilcullen, 2005, p. 607.

Section Four: Counternarcotics

U.S. counternarcotics strategies are tailored to individual countries, and U.S. counternarcotics capabilities are spread across DoS, the U.S. Department of Justice, the U.S. Department of Homeland Security, and DoD.[31]

As a result, no single government document outlines the capabilities needed to respond to the threat of drug trafficking. So, in addition to drawing on a variety of government documents, we undertook an analysis of counternarcotics operations in Mexico and Colombia. We identified the following list of "critical" functions needed for counternarcotics operations:

- Police, prosecute, and incarcerate drug traffickers.[32]
- Maintain law and order (public safety).[33]
- Integrate military and law-enforcement operational support.[34]
- Maintain border and coastal security.[35]
- Collect intelligence on narcotics traffickers.[36]
- Control corruption.[37]
- Establish drug eradication and interdiction programs.[38]
- Develop rapid and mobile reaction capabilities based on real-time intelligence.[39]
- Train civilians and military forces in counternarcotics operations.[40]
- Control roadways, airspace, and waterways.[41]

Section Five: Border and Maritime Security

If a country has porous land or maritime borders, it could become vulnerable to a myriad of security threats. The *OECD DAC Handbook on Security System Reform* provides a list of capabilities necessary for border and maritime security. In addition, the Partnership for Peace

---

[31] Section 1004 of the 1991 National Defense Authorization Act (Pub. L. 101-510) allows the U.S. military to provide specific types of support to domestic U.S. law-enforcement agencies and permits some assistance and training for foreign security forces. DoD defines four mission areas that encompass the scope of its counternarcotics program: (1) demand reduction, (2) domestic support, (3) intelligence and technology, and (4) international support. See U.S. Department of Defense, *National Drug Control Strategy: FY09 Budget Summary*, undated(b).

[32] See Schaefer, Bahney, and Riley, 2009.

[33] See Schaefer, Bahney, and Riley, 2009.

[34] U.S. Department of Defense, undated(b); U.S. Department of Defense, "Drug Interdiction and Counter Drug Activities, FY 2009 Supplemental Request," undated(a).

[35] U.S. Government Accountability Office, *Drug Control: U.S. Counternarcotics Cooperation with Venezuela Has Declined*, GAO-09-806, Washington, D.C., July 2009, p. 5.

[36] See Section 1004 of the 1991 National Defense Authorization Act (Pub. L. 101-510).

[37] See U.S. General Accounting Office, *Drug Control: Observations on U.S. Counternarcotics Activities*, statement by Henry L. Hinton, Jr., Assistant Comptroller General, National Security and International Affairs Division, GAO/T-NSIAD-98-249, Washington, D.C., 1998.

[38] U.S. Department of Defense, undated(a), undated(b).

[39] Angel Rabasa, and Peter Chalk, *Colombian Labyrinth: The Synergy of Drugs and Insurgency and Its Implications for Regional Security*, Santa Monica, Calif.: RAND Corporation, MR-1339-AF, 2001.

[40] U.S. Department of Defense, undated(a), undated(b).

[41] Rabasa and Chalk, 2001.

includes capabilities for border security and control in its ten policy priorities.[42] From these, we identified the following list of "critical" functions needed for border and maritime security operations:

- Patrol and secure land and marine borders.[43]
- Track people and goods entering and leaving the country.[44]
- Control corruption.[45]
- Coordinate with neighboring states and the international community on border security.[46]
- Collect intelligence and conduct surveillance of borders.[47]
- Train military forces on border and maritime security while border security tasks are transitioned to a nonmilitary border management agency.[48]

Section Six: Counterpiracy

The threat of piracy has increased over the past decade and has deepened understanding of the capabilities necessary for efficient and effective counterpiracy operations. We drew principally from analyses of ongoing multinational operations in the Strait of Malacca and the Horn of Africa.[49] Research institutes, such as the Congressional Research Service and the Center for Strategic and International Studies, have also published comprehensive analyses of the many issues associated with reducing piracy.[50] The International Maritime Bureau (a specialized division of the International Chamber of Commerce) and the International Maritime Organization (a UN agency) have become clearinghouses for information, training, and best practices related to counterpiracy around the world.[51]

We identified the following list of "critical" functions needed for counterpiracy operations:

- Patrol shorelines and waterways.[52]
- Respond to incidents at sea, including boarding and retaking pirated vessels.[53]

---

[42] *Partnership for Peace*, 1994; Defense Security Cooperation Agency, 2008.

[43] OECD, 2007, p. 152.

[44] OECD, 2007, p. 152.

[45] Schaefer, Bahney, and Riley, 2009.

[46] Schaefer, Bahney, and Riley, 2009.

[47] OECD, 2007, p. 152.

[48] Headquarters, U.S. Department of the Army, *Security Force Assistance*, Field Manual 3-07.1, May 2009b, p. 4-10.

[49] See Cdr Alastair Clark, Assistant Chief of Staff (Operations), Combined Maritime Forces Operations, Royal Navy, "Counter Piracy Operations, Challenges, Shortfalls and Lessons Learned," briefing, June 4, 2009.

[50] See Lauren Ploch, Christopher M. Blanchard, Ronald O'Rourke, R. Chuck Mason, and Rawle King, *Piracy Off the Horn of Africa*, R40528, Washington, D.C.: Congressional Research Service, September 28, 2009, and Jennifer Cooke, "Piracy in the Gulf of Aden," Washington, D.C.: Center for Strategic and International Studies, October 2, 2008.

[51] The International Maritime Bureau's range of antipiracy activities are available at International Chamber of Commerce, ICC Commercial Crime Services, homepage, undated. See International Maritime Organization, homepage, undated, for information about that organization.

[52] See Clark, 2009.

[53] See Clark, 2009, and U.S. National Security Council, *Countering Piracy Off the Horn of Africa: Partnership and Action Plan*, Washington, D.C., December 2008.

- Collect and analyze intelligence on pirate financing.[54]
- Conduct surveillance and reconnaissance of ships at sea.[55]
- Identify vessels arriving and departing from territorial waters.[56]
- Disrupt and dismantle pirate bases ashore.[57]
- Prosecute and incarcerate pirates.[58]
- Communicate with private vessels, international security forces, and the country's own military forces.[59]
- Coordinate with regional and international military forces.[60]
- Conduct counterpiracy training and exercises.[61]

Section Seven: Stabilize Postconflict Situations

Recent operations in Iraq and Afghanistan have underscored the importance of reducing the threat of postconflict instability. In assessing the capabilities associated with successful postconflict stabilization efforts, we examined a number of prior cases, specifically those in Liberia, Sierra Leone, East Timor, and Bosnia, and drew on a variety of published sources. RAND has been a leader in this area, producing a number of analytical reports on the security aspects of nation-building and postwar stabilization.[62] In addition to comparative studies, RAND has also produced country-specific reports that examine specific postconflict stabilization missions in great detail, for example, on rebuilding the security sector in post–civil war Liberia.[63] Several government documents, including U.S. Army Field Manual 3-07, *Stability Operations*, and the 2009 DoD Instruction 3000.05, "Stability Operations," also outline the capabilities necessary to conduct effective stability operations.[64]

---

[54] Michael Coulter, Principal Deputy Assistant Secretary of Defense for International Security Affairs, testimony before U.S. House of Representatives Armed Services Committee, March 5, 2009; U.S. National Security Council, 2008.

[55] See Clark, 2009.

[56] See Clark, 2009.

[57] U.S. National Security Council, 2008.

[58] See Clark, 2009.

[59] See Clark, 2009.

[60] See Clark, 2009.

[61] See Clark, 2009.

[62] For example, see Nora Bensahel, Olga Oliker, and Heather Peterson, *Improving Capacity for Stabilization and Reconstruction Operations*, Santa Monica, Calif.: RAND Corporation, MG-852-OSD, 2009, and Seth G. Jones, Jeremy M. Wilson, Andrew Rathmell, and K. Jack Riley, *Establishing Law and Order After Conflict*, Santa Monica, Calif.: RAND Corporation, MG-374-RC, 2005.

[63] See David Gompert, Olga Oliker, Brooke Stearns Lawson, Keith Crane, and K. Jack Riley, *Making Liberia Safe: Transformation of the National Security Sector*, Santa Monica, Calif.: RAND Corporation, MG-529-OSD, 2007.

[64] See also U.S. Senate, Committee on Foreign Relations, "Post-Conflict Nation Building," hearing, March 3, 2004, and Nina M. Serafino and Martin A. Weiss, *Peacekeeping and Post-Conflict Capabilities: The State Department's Office for Reconstruction and Stabilization*, RS22031, Washington, D.C.: Congressional Research Service, January 19, 2005.

We identified the following list of "critical" functions needed in postconflict stabilization operations:

- Maintain internal peace and security.[65]
- Ensure rule of law through an effective judicial system.[66]
- Defend against international threats.[67]
- Restore or provide basic services.[68]
- Repair critical infrastructure.[69]
- Introduce civilian control of the military.[70]
- Demobilize, disarm, and reintegrate former soldiers.[71]
- Control the proliferation of weapons.[72]

---

[65] See Jones et al., 2005, and Terrence K. Kelly, Seth G. Jones, James E. Barnett, Keith Crane, Robert C. Davis, and Carl Jensen, *A Stability Police Force for the United States: Justification and Options for Creating U.S. Capabilities*, Santa Monica, Calif.: RAND Corporation, MG-819-A, 2009.

[66] See U.S Agency for International Development, U.S. Department of Defense, U.S. Department of State, 2009, p. 3; U.S. Department of Defense Instruction 3000.05, "Stability Operations," September 16, 2009.

[67] Headquarters, U.S. Department of the Army, 2009b. p. 1-2. See also the myriad Building Partnership Capacity programs across DoD.

[68] See Headquarters, U.S. Department of the Army, *Stability Operations*, Field Manual 3-07, October 2008, p. 3-9; DoDI 3000.05, 2009.

[69] See DoDI 3000.05, 2009.

[70] See Headquarters, U.S. Department of the Army, 2008, p. 6-10, and DoDI 3000.05, 2009.

[71] See DoDI 3000.05, 2009.

[72] Defense Security Cooperation Agency, 2010.

CHAPTER THREE

The Way Ahead

The DSART can play a vital role in assisting U.S. policymakers in identifying deficiencies in a country's defense sector and then in prioritizing and allocating foreign assistance resources (see Figure 3.1).

Initial Use of the DSART

If U.S. policymakers decide that a country's defense sector will need to be assessed, they will then need to decide which assessment tools will be employed. For instance, the DSART could be used by itself or in combination with other assessment tools, such as the Criminal Justice Sector Assessment Rating Tool (CJSART).

Once it is decided that the DSART should be used to assess a country's defense sector, the next step is to determine which defense sector goals the U.S. government should seek through its foreign assistance resources. The assessor begins by answering the questions in Section One, "Characteristics of the Defense Sector." The assessor then completes those assessments that are applicable to the chosen goals. In some cases, only one of these assessments may be applicable to the country; in other cases, multiple assessments may need to be completed because the United States has multiple goals. The completed DSART assessment is then returned to U.S. policymakers, who review it and use it as background for deciding whether to undertake defense sector reforms and where to focus resources to effect the desired reforms. Initial use of the DSART provides a baseline assessment.

Figure 3.1
The Role of the DSART in Assisting Policymakers

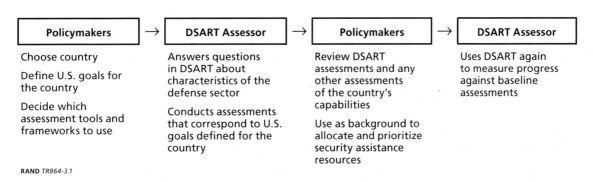

Policymakers	→	DSART Assessor	→	Policymakers	→	DSART Assessor
Choose country		Answers questions in DSART about characteristics of the defense sector		Review DSART assessments and any other assessments of the country's capabilities		Uses DSART again to measure progress against baseline assessments
Define U.S. goals for the country						
Decide which assessment tools and frameworks to use		Conducts assessments that correspond to U.S. goals defined for the country		Use as background to allocate and prioritize security assistance resources		

RAND *TR864-3.1*

Ongoing Use of the DSART

The initial assessment of a country's defense sector should be viewed as only the starting point for what will need to be a series of activities, potentially over many years, involving programs and follow-on assessments. For example, political power, social network, and stakeholder analyses will all be useful, but it will likely take months or even years of engagement to fully understand the often complex and highly sensitive relationships among officials. The DSART could be used systematically, over time, to measure progress in enhancing the capacity of the country's defense institutions and processes and in improving the country's military capabilities to respond to security threats.

The DSART, in its structured set of questions and assessments of critical defense sector capacities and of the capabilities needed to meet different types of internal security threats, is similar to the assessment tools of other U.S. government agencies and multinational organizations. The DSART does, however, lend itself to being used for a more formal and systematic assessment of these capacities and capabilities. To this end, the assessor could undertake additional steps to validate the information that is collected. For example, the assessor could answer the questions in the DSART through structured interviews or through surveys and polling of experts. To complete the evaluations, the assessor could convene workshops with a cross-section of local experts, including not only those with military or defense experience but also historians and social scientists. The assessor could employ tabletop exercises with various scenarios to evaluate the country's capabilities to respond to a range of potential internal security threats. While still qualitative, evaluations undertaken in this way would be more reliable because the assessor would be able to compare the scores from experts with different perspectives.

Moreover, historical experiences with defense sector reform in different countries suggest that approaches to planning and managing reforms need to be evolutionary, drawing on pilot programs and close monitoring over time. Initial assessments will often be, at best, a set of initial hypotheses to be tested and revised over the course of a program, especially as local capability grows. Success often depends on a commitment to learning from initiatives and revisiting initial assumptions and strategies. Thus, any initial DSART assessment must be viewed in this light and serve not only as one input into government decisionmaking but also as the starting point for continuing efforts to reform a country's defense sector.

Evolution of the DSART

The DSART could be used by countries other than the United States in assessing either their own defense sector capabilities or those of countries to which they are providing assistance. The DSART could also be used by multilateral organizations to assess the countries to which they are or may wish to provide assistance. In addition, it could be used as it is currently structured, or it could be revised to take into account different views of, for example, the "critical" capacities of a defense sector.

While the DSART is now ready for use, U.S. goals for defense sector reform may evolve. The DSART is designed with a flexible architecture so that it can be adapted to a changing security environment. For instance, the DSART can accommodate additional assessment sections as new foreign assistance goals arise or if policymakers are interested in assessing a country's capability to address a security issue that is not presently included in the tool. In addition, to maximize its utility, the DSART was designed to be flexible enough to assess defense sectors in varying degrees of development, from failing states to well-developed democracies.

Our goal is that the tool will continue to evolve as it is used in different countries and with different goals in mind.

Compilation of Assessment Tools

USAID's SSR Assessment Framework, ICAF, CJSART, and the DIB Assessment

In addition to the *OECD DAC Handbook*, we found the following tools to be particularly informative in the development of the DSART:

- USAID's SSR Assessment Framework
- The DoS Office of Reconstruction and Development's ICAF
- The DoS Bureau for International Narcotics and Law Enforcement Affairs CJSART
- DoD's WIF DIB Assessment Methodology.

USAID's Security Sector Reform Assessment Framework

With USAID in the lead, the U.S. government is currently developing its SSR Assessment Framework that will serve as a consistent overarching, interagency framework for SSR assessments. Ultimately, subsector assessment tools, such as the DSART and the CJSART, will nest under the SSR Assessment Framework. We were kept updated on the status of the USAID SSR Assessment Framework, and we incorporated the key principles in the draft version into the DSART, particularly its emphasis on local context, institutions, and stakeholders.

The Interagency Conflict Assessment Framework

The purpose of the ICAF is to "develop a commonly held understanding, across relevant [U.S. government] Departments and Agencies of the dynamics driving and mitigating violent conflict within a country, that informs US policy and planning decisions."[1] Furthermore, "[i]n whole-of-government crisis response under the Interagency Management System for Reconstruction and Stabilization, an ICAF analysis normally will be part of the strategic planning process led by the Country Reconstruction and Stabilization Group Secretariat."[2]

The ICAF is composed of two major components: the "Conflict Diagnosis" and the "Segue into Planning." The first task in conducting an ICAF analysis is diagnosing the conflict. There are four steps in this process: (1) evaluate the context of the conflict, (2) understand core grievances and social or institutional resilience, (3) identify drivers of conflict and mitigating factors, and (4) describe opportunities for increasing or decreasing conflict.[3] The findings of the conflict diagnosis then feed into the planning process.

---

[1] U.S. Department of State, Office of the Coordinator for Reconstruction and Development, 2008, p. 2.

[2] U.S. Department of State, Office of the Coordinator for Reconstruction and Development, 2008, p. 5.

[3] U.S. Department of State, Office of the Coordinator for Reconstruction and Development, 2008, p. 6.

We incorporated all four steps of the ICAF conflict diagnosis into the DSART. We felt that to conduct a comprehensive assessment of the defense sector, an assessor must understand the context of the country, its institutions, drivers of conflict, and opportunities for increasing or decreasing conflict. By understanding the context of current or previous conflicts, policymakers can make better decisions regarding how to allocate resources or which areas should be targeted for reform.

The Criminal Justice Sector Assessment Rating Tool

The CJSART defines the criminal justice sector as follows:[4]

- laws, including a nation's criminal code and criminal procedure code
- judicial institutions, including judges, public prosecution, and the defense bar for both private attorneys and public defenders
- law enforcement, including policing, investigations, and forensics
- border security (land, marine, and air), including customs and monitoring of points of entry
- corrections system, including the prison system and detention facilities
- international cooperation, including treaties relevant to criminal justice to which a nation is a signatory and membership or participation in conventions, agreements, and international organizations.

The CJSART asks more than 700 questions about these six areas, including a series of contextual questions and a series of yes/no measurement indicators related to specific functions (e.g., Is there a criminal code? Is there a separation of powers between the judiciary and the other branches of government?). Depending on how many questions an assessor answers in the affirmative, he or she assigns a numeric ranking that shows the stage of development of various aspects of a criminal justice system. For instance, if a country meets between 0 and 20 percent of a certain performance capability, it is ranked as a Level 1; 21–40 percent is Level 2, 41–60 percent is Level 3, 61–80 percent is Level 4, and 81–100 percent is Level 5 for that specific capability.[5] In addition, certain fundamental U.S. government priority indicators must be met for a country to score above Level 2 in any performance capability.[6]

The CJSART was a major step forward in the art of security sector assessments because the standardized structure of the tool allows for the systematic evaluation of the criminal justice sector and for progress to be tracked over time. Prior to the CJSART, the status of a country's criminal justice system was often determined through consideration of an ad hoc, often expedient assortment of considerations or via the personal expertise of individual program managers. Because the collection of factors considered was neither consistent nor always reflective of U.S. government assistance priorities, it was often not possible to affirm definitively when progress was made in a state's a criminal justice system.[7] The CJSART has advanced the field's ability to reliably and systematically evaluate criminal justice sector assistance.

---

[4]   U.S. Department of State, Bureau for International Narcotics and Law Enforcement Affairs, 2008, pp. 4–5.

[5]   U.S. Department of State, Bureau for International Narcotics and Law Enforcement Affairs, 2008, p. 6.

[6]   U.S. Department of State, Bureau for International Narcotics and Law Enforcement Affairs, 2008, p. 7.

[7]   U.S. Department of State, Bureau for International Narcotics and Law Enforcement Affairs, 2008, p. 5.

Warsaw Initiative Fund Defense Institution Building Assessment Methodology

Finally, we found DoD's WIF DIB Assessment Methodology to be quite useful in identifying questions that were relevant to particular aspects of defense sector reform (e.g., professional military education, logistics). The DIB Assessment Methodology asks very specific questions related to defense policy, including policy and strategy, democratic control of the armed forces, defense budgeting, human resource management, logistics, border security, peacekeeping, and professional military education. Since the methodology is designed to assess relatively developed defense sectors, its questions were helpful as we thought through the topics that needed to be addressed when assessing both nascent and more developed defense sectors.

DoD and NATO Assessment Tools Used in Iraq and Afghanistan

We also consulted the various assessment tools that DoD and NATO developed for use in assessing security forces in Iraq and Afghanistan. For instance, the Afghan National Army Training Readiness Assessment Tool (ATRAT) informed questions in the DSART related to military readiness. The ATRAT is similar to the U.S. Army's Unit Status Report and it provides a scorecard for assessing Afghan National Army units along six dimensions:

- personnel
- command and control
- training
- sustainment and logistics
- equipment on hand
- equipment readiness.

Many of the assessments used in Iraq and Afghanistan focused on assessing individual military and police units. Such individual-level assessment tools could be used in conjunction with the DSART.

Other Assessment Tools Used by the U.S. Government

We consulted the following additional tools used by the U.S. government to inform the development of the DSART:

- Linn Hammergren, "Assessments, Monitoring, Evaluation, and Research: Improving the Knowledge Base for Judicial Reform Programs," United Nations Development Programme, undated.
- U.S. Agency for International Development, *Conducting a Conflict Assessment: A Framework for Strategy and Program Development*, Washington, D.C., April 2005.
- U.S. Agency for International Development, *Corruption Assessment Handbook*, Washington, D.C., May 2006.
- U.S. Agency for International Development, *Decentralization and Democratic Local Governance Programming Handbook*, Washington, D.C., May 2000.

- U.S. Agency for International Development, *Guide to Rule of Law Country Analysis: The Rule of Law Strategic Framework*, Washington, D.C., August 2008.
- U.S. Agency for International Development, Tactical Conflict Assessment Framework.[8]
- U.S. Agency for International Development, *The Role of Media in a Democracy: A Strategic Approach*, Washington, D.C., June 1999.
- U.S. Agency for International Development, *Tools for Assessing Corruption and Integrity Institutions: A Handbook*, Washington, D.C., August 2005.
- U.S. Agency for International Development, *Measuring Fragility: Indicators and Method for Rating State Performance*, Washington, D.C., June 2005.
- U.S. Agency for International Development, *Handbook of Democracy and Governance Program Indicators*, Washington, D.C., August 1998.
- U.S. Agency for International Development, *Conducting a DG Assessment: A Framework for Strategy Development*, Washington, D.C., November 2000.
- Peacekeeping and Stability Operations Institute, "Security Sector Reform in Liberia Part 1: An Assessment of Defense Reform," Carlisle, Pa., July 2008.

Assessment Tools Used by Foreign Governments or International Organizations

During the development of the DSART, we considered the following assessment tools that are currently used by other countries and international organizations:

- International Security Assistance Force (ISAF) Afghan Training Readiness Assessment Tool. "Measuring ANSF Capabilities Through Milestones," overview of ISAF Afghan Training Readiness Tool, *The Enduring Ledger* (Combined Security Transition Command–Afghanistan), April 2009, p. 18.
- Nicole Ball, Tsjeard Bouta, and Luc van de Goor, *Enhancing Democratic Governance of the Security Sector: An Institutional Assessment Framework*, Clingendael Institute for the Netherlands Ministry of Foreign Affairs, 2003.
- Organization of American States, Inter-American Drug Abuse Control Commission, *Multilateral Evaluation Mechanism*, 2007–2009.
- Nicola Popovich, "Security Sector Reform Assessment, Monitoring and Evaluation and Gender," in Megan Bastick and Kristin Valasek, eds., *Gender and Security Sector Reform Toolkit*, Geneva: Geneva Centre for the Democratic Control of Armed Forces, 2008.
- Dory Reiling, Linn Hammergren, and Adrian Di Giovanni, *Justice Sector Assessments: A Handbook,* Washington, D.C.: World Bank, 2008.
- Christopher Stone, "Developing Justice Indicators," presentation to the Inter-American Development Bank, January 12, 2005.
- Swedish International Development Cooperation Agency, *Manual for Conflict Analysis: Methods Document*, Stockholm: Division for Peace and Security Through Development Cooperation, January 2006.
- UK Department for International Development, "Understanding and Supporting Security Sector Reform," London, 2002.

---

[8]   See description at U.S. Agency for International Development, 2008b.

- Robert Nash, Alan Hudson, and Cecilia Lutrell, *Mapping Political Context Online Toolkit: A Toolkit for Civil Society Organisations*, London: UK Overseas Development Institute, July 2006.
- United Nations Office of the High Commissioner for Human Rights, *Rule of Law Tools for Post-Conflict States: Mapping the Justice Sector*, New York and Geneva, 2006.
- United Nations Office on Drugs and Crime, *Criminal Justice Assessment Toolkit*, New York, 2006.
- United Nations Office on Drugs and Crime, *The Application of the United Nations Standards and Norms in Crime Prevention and Criminal Justice*, February 2003.
- Suzanne Verstegen, Luc van de Goor, and Jeroen de Zeeuw, *The Stability Assessment Framework: Designing Integrated Responses for Security, Governance and Development*, Clingendael Institute for the Netherlands Ministry of Foreign Affairs, 2005.

Assessment Tools Used by NGOs

Finally, we took into account several tools used by NGOs:

- Association of the U.S. Army and Center for Strategic and International Studies, *Post-Conflict Reconstruction: Task Framework*, May 2002.
- David Bruce and Rachel Neild, *The Police That We Want: A Handbook for Oversight of Police in South Africa*, Johannesburg, South Africa: Centre for the Study of Violence and Reconciliation, 2005.
- Human Rights Centre, "Democratic Audit: The Assessment Framework," undated.
- "Conducting an Assessment," in Coleen Rausch, ed., *Combating Serious Crimes in Post-conflict Societies: A Handbook for Policymakers and Practitioners*, Washington, D.C.: United States Institute of Peace, 2006.
- Vera Institute of Justice, *Measuring Progress Towards Safety and Justice: A Global Guide to the Design of Performance Indicators Across the Justice Sector*, New York, November 2003.

Bibliography

Anders, David P., *Developing an Operational Level Strategic Communication Model for Counterinsurgency*, Carlisle, Pa.: Center for Strategic Leadership, U.S. Army War College, February 24, 2009.

Association of the U.S. Army and Center for Strategic and International Studies, *Post-Conflict Reconstruction: Task Framework*, May 2002. As of March 24, 2010:
http://www.csis.org/images/stories/pcr/framework.pdf

Ball, Nicole, Tsjeard Bouta, and Luc van de Goor, *Enhancing Democratic Governance of the Security Sector: An Institutional Assessment Framework*, Clingendael Institute for the Netherlands Ministry of Foreign Affairs, 2003. As of March 24, 2010:
http://www.clingendael.nl/publications/2003/20030800_cru_paper_ball.pdf

Beers, Jason, *Community Oriented Policing and Counterinsurgency: A Conceptual Model*, thesis, Ft. Leavenworth, Kan.: U.S. Army Command and Staff College, 2007.

Bensahel, Nora, Olga Oliker, and Heather Peterson, *Improving Capacity for Stabilization and Reconstruction Operations*, Santa Monica, Calif.: RAND Corporation, MG-852-OSD, 2009. As of March 24, 2010:
http://www.rand.org/pubs/monographs/MG852/

Bruce, David, and Rachel Neild, *The Police That We Want: A Handbook for Oversight of Police in South Africa*, Johannesburg, South Africa: Centre for the Study of Violence and Reconciliation, 2005.

Byman, Daniel L., "Friends Like These: Counterinsurgency and the War on Terrorism," *International Security*, Vol. 31, No. 2, Fall 2006, pp. 79–115.

Clark, Cdr Alastair, Assistant Chief of Staff (Operations), Combined Maritime Forces, Royal Navy, "Counter Piracy Operations, Challenges, Shortfalls and Lessons Learned," briefing, June 4, 2009. As of March 24, 2010:
http://www.nato.int/structur/AC/141/pdf/PS-M/Combined%20Maritime%20Forces%20Ops.pdf

Cole, Eden, Kerstin Eppert, and Katrin Kinzelbach, eds., *Public Oversight of the Security Sector: A Handbook for Civil Society Organizations*, Geneva: Geneva Centre for the Democratic Control of Armed Forces, 2008. As of March 24, 2010:
http://www.dcaf.ch/publications/kms/details.cfm?ord279=title&q279=Public+Oversight&lng=en&id=95396&nav1=5

"Conducting an Assessment," in Coleen Rausch, ed., *Combating Serious Crimes in Postconflict Societies: A Handbook for Policymakers and Practitioners*, Washington, D.C.: United States Institute of Peace, 2006.

Cooke, Jennifer, "Piracy in the Gulf of Aden," Washington, D.C.: Center for Strategic and International Studies, October 2, 2008.

Corum, James, *Training Indigenous Forces for Counterinsurgency: A Tale of Two Insurgencies*, Carlisle, Pa.: Strategic Studies Institute, U.S. Army War College, March 2006.

Coulter, Michael, Principal Deputy Assistant Secretary of Defense for International Security Affairs, testimony before the House of Representatives Armed Services Committee, March 5, 2009.

Defense Security Cooperation Agency, *Fiscal Year (FY) 2009 Budget Estimates*, Washington, D.C., February 2008. As of March 24, 2010:
http://comptroller.defense.gov/defbudget/fy2009/budget_justification/pdfs/01_Operation_and_Maintenance/O_M_VOL_1_PARTS/DSCA%20FY%202009%20PB%20OP-5.pdf

———, *Fiscal Year 2011 Budget Estimates*, Washington, D.C., February 2010. As of March 24, 2010:
http://comptroller.defense.gov/defbudget/fy2011/budget_justification/pdfs/01_Operation_and_Maintenance/O_M_VOL_1_PARTS/DSCA_FY11.pdf

DoDI—*see* U.S. Department of Defense Instruction.

Gompert, David, John Gordon IV, Adam Grissom, David R. Frelinger, Seth G. Jones, Martin C. Libicki, Edward O'Connell, Brooke Stearns Lawson, and Robert E. Hunter, *War by Other Means—Building Complete and Balanced Capabilities for Counterinsurgency: RAND Counterinsurgency Study—Final Report*, Santa Monica, Calif.: RAND Corporation, MG-595/2-OSD, 2008. As of March 24, 2010:
http://www.rand.org/pubs/monographs/MG595.2/

Gompert, David C., Terrence K. Kelly, Brooke Stearns Lawson, Michelle Parker, and Kimberly Colloton, *Reconstruction Under Fire: Unifying Civil and Military Counterinsurgency*, Santa Monica, Calif.: RAND Corporation, MG-870-OSD, 2009. As of March 24, 2010:
http://www.rand.org/pubs/monographs/MG870/

Gompert, David C., Olga Oliker, Brooke Stearns Lawson, Keith Crane, and K. Jack Riley, *Making Liberia Safe: Transformation of the National Security Sector*, Santa Monica, Calif.: RAND Corporation, MG-529-OSD, 2007. As of March 24, 2010:
http://www.rand.org/pubs/monographs/MG529/

Gompert, David C., Olga Oliker, and Anga R. Timilsina, *Clean, Lean, and Able: A Strategy for Defense Development*, Santa Monica, Calif.: RAND Corporation, OP-101-RC, 2004. As of March 24, 2010:
http://www.rand.org/pubs/occasional_papers/OP101/

Hammergren, Linn, "Assessments, Monitoring, Evaluation, and Research: Improving the Knowledge Base for Judicial Reform Programs," United Nations Development Programme, undated. As of March 24, 2010:
http://www.pogar.org/publications/judiciary/linn1/knowledge.pdf

Headquarters, U.S. Department of the Army, *Counterinsurgency*, Field Manual 3-24, Washington, D.C., December 16, 2006.

———, *Stability Operations*, Field Manual 3-07, Washington, D.C., October 2008.

———, *Tactics in Counterinsurgency*, Field Manual 3-07.2, Washington, D.C., April 2009a.

———, *Security Force Assistance*, Field Manual 3-07.1, Washington, D.C., May 2009b.

Hermsmeyer, COL Gregory, "Security Sector Reform: DoD Guidance, Organization and Authorities," briefing, undated.

Human Rights Centre, "Democratic Audit: The Assessment Framework," undated. As of March 24, 2010:
http://www.democraticaudit.com/auditing_democracy/assessmentframework.php

International Chamber of Commerce, ICC Commercial Crime Services, homepage, undated. As of March 24, 2010:
http://www.icc-ccs.org/

International Maritime Organization, homepage, undated. As of March 24, 2010:
http://www.imo.org/

Jones, Seth G., Jeremy M. Wilson, Andrew Rathmell, and K. Jack Riley, *Establishing Law and Order After Conflict*, Santa Monica, Calif.: RAND Corporation, MG-374-RC, 2005. As of March 24, 2010:
http://www.rand.org/pubs/monographs/MG374/

Kelly, Terrence K., Seth G. Jones, James E. Barnett, Keith Crane, Robert C. Davis, and Carl Jensen, *A Stability Police Force for the United States: Justification and Options for Creating U.S. Capabilities*, Santa Monica, Calif.: RAND Corporation, MG-819-A, 2009. As of March 24, 2010:
http://www.rand.org/pubs/monographs/MG819/

Kilcullen, David J., "Countering Global Insurgency," *Journal of Strategic Studies*, Vol. 28, No. 4, August 2005, pp. 597–617.

"Measuring ANSF Capabilities Through Milestones," *The Enduring Ledger* (Combined Security Transition Command–Afghanistan), April 2009, p. 18. As of June 28, 2010:
http://www.cstc-a.com/News/enduring%20ledgers/2009endledger/ApriEL.pdf

Moroney, Jennifer D. P., Jefferson P. Marquis, Cathryn Quantic Thurston, and Gregory F. Treverton, *A Framework to Assess Programs for Building Partnerships*, Santa Monica, Calif.: RAND Corporation, MG-863-OSD, 2009. As of March 24, 2010:
http://www.rand.org/pubs/monographs/MG863/

Nash, Robert, Alan Hudson, and Cecilia Lutrell, *Mapping Political Context: A Toolkit for Civil Society Organisations*, London: UK Overseas Development Institute, July 2006. As of March 24, 2010:
http://www.odi.org.uk/resources/details.asp?id=152&title=mapping-political-context-toolkit-civil-society-organisations

OECD—*see* Organisation for Economic Co-Operation and Development.

Organisation for Economic Co-Operation and Development, *Security Sector Reform and Governance*, Paris, 2005.

———, *OECD DAC Handbook on Security System Reform: Supporting Security and Justice*, Paris, 2007.

Organization of American States, Inter-American Drug Abuse Control Commission, *Multilateral Evaluation Mechanism*, 2007–2009. As of March 24, 2010:
http://www.cicad.oas.org/MEM/ENG/Questionnaires/Fifth%20Round/index.asp

Partnership for Peace: Framework Document Issued by the Heads of State and Government Participating in the Meeting of the North Atlantic Council, Brussels, January 10, 1994.

Peacekeeping and Stability Operations Institute, "Security Sector Reform in Liberia Part 1: An Assessment of Defense Reform," Carlisle, Pa., July 2008. As of March 24, 2010:
http://pksoi.army.mil/srt/documents/Perspectives_SSR%20in%20Liberia%20Pt1.pdf

Ploch, Lauren, Christopher M. Blanchard, Ronald O'Rourke, R. Chuck Mason, and Rawle O. King, *Piracy Off the Horn of Africa*, R40528, Washington, D.C.: Congressional Research Service, September 28, 2009.

Popovich, Nicola, "Security Sector Reform Assessment, Monitoring and Evaluation and Gender," in Megan Bastick and Kristin Valasek, eds., *Gender and Security Sector Reform Toolkit*, Geneva: Geneva Centre for the Democratic Control of Armed Forces, 2008.

Public Law 87-195, Foreign Assistance Act of 1961, September 4, 1961.

Public Law 101-510, National Defense Authorization Act for Fiscal Year 1991, November 5, 1990.

Rabasa, Angel, and Peter Chalk, *Colombian Labyrinth: The Synergy of Drugs and Insurgency and Its Implications for Regional Security*, Santa Monica, Calif.: RAND Corporation, MR-1339-AF, 2001. As of March 24, 2010:
http://www.rand.org/pubs/monograph_reports/MR1339/

Reiling, Dory, Linn Hammergren, and Adrian Di Giovanni, *Justice Sector Assessments: A Handbook*, Washington, D.C.: World Bank, 2008. As of March 24, 2010:
http://web.worldbank.org/WBSITE/EXTERNAL/TOPICS/EXTLAWJUSTINST/0,,contentMDK:2125784
3-pagePK:148956-piPK:216618-theSitePK:1974062,00.html

Schaefer, Agnes Gereben, Benjamin Bahney, and K. Jack Riley, *Security in Mexico: Implications for U.S. Policy Options*, Santa Monica, Calif.: RAND Corporation, MG-876-RC, 2009. As of March 24, 2010:
http://www.rand.org/pubs/monographs/MG876/

Serafino, Nina M., and Martin A. Weiss, *Peacekeeping and Post-Conflict Capabilities: The State Department's Office for Reconstruction and Stabilization*, RS22031, Washington, D.C.: Congressional Research Service, January 19, 2005.

Stone, Christopher, "Developing Justice Indicators," presentation to the Inter-American Development Bank, January 12, 2005.

Swedish International Development Cooperation Agency, *Manual for Conflict Analysis: Methods Document*, Stockholm: Division for Peace and Security Through Development Cooperation, January 2006.

UK Department for International Development, "Understanding and Supporting Security Sector Reform," London, 2002.

United Nations Office of the High Commissioner for Human Rights, *Rule of Law Tools for Post-Conflict States: Mapping the Justice Sector*, HR/PUB/06/2, New York and Geneva, 2006. As of March 24, 2010:
http://www.unhcr.org/refworld/docid/46ceb9582.html

United Nations Office on Drugs and Crime, *The Application of the United Nations Standards and Norms in Crime Prevention and Criminal Justice*, February 2003.

———, *Criminal Justice Assessment Toolkit*, New York, 2006. As of March 24, 2010:
http://www.unodc.org/documents/justice-and-prison-reform/cjat_eng/Introducing_the_Toolkit.pdf

United Nations Security Council, report of the Secretary-General on the situation in Somalia, S/2009/373, July 20, 2009.

U.S. Agency for International Development, *Handbook of Democracy and Governance Program Indicators*, Washington, D.C., August 1998. As of March 24, 2010:
http://www.usaid.gov/our_work/democracy_and_governance/publications/pdfs/pnacc390.pdf

———, *The Role of Media in a Democracy: A Strategic Approach*, Washington, D.C., June 1999. As of March 24, 2010:
http://www.usaid.gov/our_work/democracy_and_governance/publications/pdfs/pnace630.pdf

———, *Decentralization and Democratic Local Governance Programming Handbook*, May 2000a. As of March 24, 2010:
http://www.usaid.gov/our_work/democracy_and_governance/publications/pdfs/pnach300.pdf

———, *Conducting a DG Assessment: A Framework for Strategy Development*, Washington, D.C., November 2000b. As of March 24, 2010:
http://www.usaid.gov/our_work/democracy_and_governance/publications/pdfs/pnach305.pdf

———, *Conducting a Conflict Assessment: A Framework for Strategy and Program Development*, Washington, D.C.: April 2005a.

———, *Measuring Fragility: Indicators and Methods for Rating State Performance*, Washington, D.C., June 2005b. As of March 24, 2010:
http://pdf.dec.org/pdf_docs/PNADD462.pdf

———, *Tools for Assessing Corruption and Integrity Institutions: A Handbook*, Washington, D.C., August 2005c. As of March 24, 2010:
http://www.irisprojects.umd.edu/anticorruption/Files/IRIS_Assessment_Handbook.pdf

———, *Corruption Assessment Handbook*, Washington, D.C., May 2006. As of March 24, 2010:
http://www1.worldbank.org/publicsector/anticorrupt/USAIDCorAsmtHandbook.pdf

———, *Guide to Rule of Law Country Analysis: The Rule of Law Strategic Framework*, Washington, D.C., August 2008a. As of March 24, 2010:
http://www.usaid.gov/our_work/democracy_and_governance/publications/pdfs/ROL_Strategic_Framework_Sept_08.pdf

———, "Tactical Conflict Assessment Framework," web page, last updated August 11, 2008b. As of March 24, 2010:
http://www.usaid.gov/our_work/global_partnerships/ma/tcaf.html

———, "USG SSR Assessment Framework," February 2, 2009.

U.S. Agency for International Development, U.S. Department of Defense, and U.S. Department of State, *Security Sector Reform*, Washington, D.C., 2009. As of March 24, 2010:
http://www.usaid.gov/our_work/democracy_and_governance/publications/pdfs/SSR_JS_Mar2009.pdf

U.S. Central Intelligence Agency, "Guide to the Analysis of Insurgency," Washington, D.C., January 5, 2009.

U.S. Department of Defense, "Drug Interdiction and Counter Drug Activities, FY 2009 Supplemental Request," undated(a). As of March 24, 2010:
http://comptroller.defense.gov/defbudget/fy2009/Supplemental/FY2009_Supplemental_Request/pdfs/operation/081_Counternarcotics_FY09Supp.pdf

———, *National Drug Control Strategy: FY09 Budget Summary*, undated(b). As of March 24, 2010:
http://www.whitehousedrugpolicy.gov/publications/policy/09budget/defense.pdf

———, "Warsaw Initiative Fund Defense Institution Building Assessment Methodology," undated(c).

———, *Fiscal Year 2010 Budget Request, Summary Justification*, May 2009. As of June 28, 2010:
http://comptroller.defense.gov/defbudget/fy2010/fy2010_SSJ.pdf

U.S. Department of Defense Instruction 3000.05, "Stability Operations," September 16, 2009.

U.S. Department of State, "Foreign Assistance Standardized Program Structure and Definitions," January 2010. As of March 24, 2010:
http://www.state.gov/documents/organization/136594.pdf

U.S. Department of State, Bureau for International Narcotics and Law Enforcement Affairs, *Criminal Justice Sector Assessment Rating Tool: A U.S. Government Interagency Framework to Assess the Capacity of International Criminal Justice Systems*, Washington, D.C., January 2008.

U.S. Department of State, Office of the Coordinator for Reconstruction and Development, *Interagency Conflict Assessment Framework*, Washington, D.C., 2008.

U.S. General Accounting Office, *Drug Control: Observations on U.S. Counternarcotics Activities*, statement by Henry L. Hinton, Jr., Assistant Comptroller General, National Security and International Affairs Division, GAO/T-NSIAD-98-249, Washington, D.C., September 16, 1998.

U.S. Government Accountability Office, *Drug Control: U.S. Counternarcotics Cooperation with Venezuela Has Declined*, GAO-09-806, Washington, D.C., July 2009.

U.S. National Security Council, *Countering Piracy Off the Horn of Africa: Partnership and Action Plan*, Washington, D.C., December 2008. As of March 24, 2010:
http://www.marad.dot.gov/documents/Countering_Piracy_Off_The_Horn_of_Africa_-_Partnership__Action_Plan.pdf

U.S. Senate, Committee on Foreign Relations, "Post-Conflict Nation Building," hearing, March 3, 2004.

———, "Confronting Piracy Off the Coast of Somalia," hearing, April 30, 2009.

Vera Institute of Justice, *Measuring Progress Towards Safety and Justice: A Global Guide to the Design of Performance Indicators Across the Justice Sector*, New York, November 2003. As of March 24, 2010:
http://www.vera.org/download?file=9/207_404.pdf

Verstegen, Suzanne, Luc van de Goor, and Jeroen de Zeeuw, *The Stability Assessment Framework: Designing Integrated Responses for Security, Governance and Development*, Clingendael Institute for the Netherlands Ministry of Foreign Affairs, 2005.

Defense Sector Assessment
Rating Tool

Prepared for the Office of the Secretary of Defense

Approved for public release; distribution unlimited

RAND | NATIONAL DEFENSE RESEARCH INSTITUTE

About the DSART

Defense Sector Assessment Rating Tool (DSART) consists of six assessments to qualitatively and quantitatively determine the state of a country's defense sector, its institutions and processes, and its capacity to carry out operations for counterterrorism and counterinsurgency, counternarcotics, border and maritime security, counterpiracy, and postconflict stabilization. While the DSART is ready for use, U.S. goals for defense sector reform may evolve, so it is designed with a flexible architecture that can be adapted to a changing security environment.

For more information about the development, structure, application, and potential evolution of the DSART, see *Developing a Defense Sector Assessment Rating Tool*, by Agnes Gereben Schaefer, Lynn E. Davis, Ely Ratner, Molly Dunigan, Jeremiah Goulka, Heather Peterson, and K. Jack Riley, Santa Monica, Calif.: RAND Corporation, TR-864-OSD, 2010, which is available online at http://www.rand.org/pubs/technical_reports/TR864/.

The research that produced the DSART was sponsored by the Office of the Secretary of Defense and the Defense Security Cooperation Agency and conducted within the International Security and Defense Policy Center of the RAND National Defense Research Institute, a federally funded research and development center sponsored by the Office of the Secretary of Defense, the Joint Staff, the Unified Combatant Commands, the Navy, the Marine Corps, the defense agencies, and the defense Intelligence Community.

Questions or comments are welcome and may be directed to the project co-leaders:

Agnes Gereben Schaefer
RAND Corporation
4570 Fifth Avenue, Suite 600
Pittsburgh, PA 15213
(412) 683-2300 x4488
Agnes_Schaefer@rand.org

Lynn E. Davis
RAND Corporation
1200 South Hayes Street
Arlington, VA 22202
(703) 413-1100 x5399
Lynn_Davis@rand.org

More information about RAND is available at www.rand.org.

Contents

Introduction

Background

The U.S. Department of Defense (DoD) has a number of assistance programs to build the capacity of foreign partners in order to promote a variety of different U.S. security goals.

One overall goal could be to support a country in its efforts to reform its defense institutions and processes in ways to reflect what the United States views as important for effective military planning and operations, e.g., civilian control of the military, military professionalism. Through such efforts, the country would be better able to manage its own security problems and potentially partner with the United States and other countries in international military operations.

Another set of goals could be to improve a country's capability to counter specific internal security threats, such as terrorism and insurgency, drug trafficking, porous land or sea borders, piracy, and instability in the aftermath of a conflict.

An understanding of a country's defense sector can help policymakers promote any or all of these goals, as well as prioritize DoD programs and allocate scarce resources for an individual country or among different countries. The Defense Sector Assessment Rating Tool (DSART) is designed to provide policymakers with such an understanding.

For the purposes of this tool, the defense sector in a country is defined as the uniformed military plus the military and civilian management, accountability, and oversight systems, mechanisms, and processes that sustain it.

The DSART begins with a section that asks a series of questions. The answers to these questions provide an understanding of the general characteristics of the defense sector in the country. This provides background for undertaking the assessments in the six sections that follow.

The questions in Section One (Characteristics of the Defense Sector) focus first on the military forces themselves and then on the various institutions and processes that sustain and exercise control over them. The section ends with questions aimed at understanding the country's overall political, economic, and security environment. What the assessor is seeking through these questions is a general understanding of the defense sector in the country and enough information for the assessments that follow.

Section Two (Defense Institutions and Processes) involves an assessment of how the country's institutions and processes match what the United States views as the "critical" capacities of a defense sector. These critical capacities are derived from U.S. government documents that address defense and security sector reform.

This assessment involves a qualitative appraisal and then a quantitative scoring of the country's capacities, on a scale of 1 (entirely lacking) to 5 (strong and no major improvement needed). Having revealed where deficiencies exist, Section Two then poses a series of questions. The answers to these questions provide an overall assessment of the prospects in the country for reforming those areas in which deficiencies were found.

The next five sections of the DSART focus on specific internal security threats and involve an assessment of the country's capabilities for responding:

- Section Three (Counterterrorism and Counterinsurgency)
- Section Four (Counternarcotics)
- Section Five (Border and Maritime Security)
- Section Six (Counterpiracy)
- Section Seven (Stabilize Postconflict Situations).

Each section includes a series of questions. The answers to these questions provide an assessment of the country's overall capabilities to respond to the specific threat. The answers serve as a basis for an assessment of the country's capabilities to carry out the "critical" functions necessary to respond to each of the specific types of security threat. Again, the assessment involves a qualitative appraisal and then quantitative scoring. Each section ends with an assessment of the country's prospects for improving its capabilities in the areas in which deficiencies were found.

How to Use the DSART

The U.S. government has a number of assessment tools, e.g., the Criminal Justice Sector Assessment Rating Tool. The DSART could be used in conjunction with other tools or on its own.

Once a country is chosen for a defense sector assessment, the next step for policymakers is to specify their reasons for wanting such an assessment as well as the potential goals the United States has for the country.

With that guidance, the assessor then begins to use the DSART. In *all* cases, the assessor answers the questions in Section One (Characteristics of the Defense Sector). Then, depending on the potential goals for the country, the assessor completes the assessment in the subsequent section or sections of the DSART. For example, if the goal is to reform the country's defense institutions and processes, the assessor would complete the assessment in Section Two. If the goal is to improve the country's counterterrorism capabilities, the assessor would complete the assessment in Section Three. If the United States has multiple goals in the country, then the assessor would complete multiple assessments in the appropriate sections.

The DSART may not include all the security goals the United States might have for a country. However, the architecture of the tool is flexible enough to allow an assessor to introduce additional questions and sections.

The DSART provides a baseline assessment of the defense sector in a country. The initial assessment of a country's defense sector should be viewed as only the starting point for what will be a series of activities, potentially over many years, that will involve programs and follow-on assessments. For example, political power, social network, and stakeholder analyses will all be useful, but it will likely take months or even years of engagement to fully understand the often complex and highly sensitive relationships among officials. So, the DSART could be used systematically, over time, to measure progress in enhancing the capacities of the country's defense institutions and processes and improving the country's military capabilities to respond to security threats.

The DSART, in its structured set of questions and assessments of critical defense sector capacities and of the capabilities needed to meet different types of internal security threats, is similar to the assessment tools of other U.S. government agencies and multinational organizations. The DSART does, however, lend itself to being used for a more formal and systematic assessment of these capacities and capabilities. To this end, the assessor could take additional steps to validate the information that is collected, e.g., answering the questions in the DSART through structured interviews, using workshops with a cross-section of local experts, or conducting tabletop exercises for the qualitative evaluations.

Moreover, historical experiences with defense sector reform in different countries suggest that approaches to planning and managing reforms need to be evolutionary, drawing on pilot programs and close monitoring over time. Thus, initial assessments will often be, at best, a set of initial hypotheses to be tested and revised over the course of a program, especially as local capability grows. Success often depends on a commitment to learning from initiatives and revisiting initial assumptions and strategies. Any initial DSART assessment must be viewed in this light and serve not only as one input into government decisionmaking but also as the starting point for continuing efforts to reform a country's defense sector.

Characteristics of the Defense Sector

This section poses a series of questions. The answers to these questions provide an understanding of the characteristics of the defense sector in the country. This information serves as background for undertaking the assessments in the sections of the DSART that follow. The questions focus first on the military forces and then on the various institutions and processes that sustain and exercise control over them. The section ends with questions aimed at providing the context for the assessment of the defense sector in terms of understanding the country's overall political, economic, and security environment.

I. Military Forces

A. Role of the Military

What is the role of the military in society? Has it changed over time?

What roles and responsibilities does the military have, and what functions does it carry out? Are they codified in law? What are the major challenges faced by the military?

Does the military have peacetime internal security responsibilities and functions, and, if so, what are they? Are they distinguished from those of the national and local police? How are the respective responsibilities managed, coordinated, and resourced? Are there any overlaps, ambiguities, and redundancies?

Is there a gendarme-type force? Are its roles and authorities clearly understood? If not, who fills the role of the gendarme?

Does the country have paramilitary or other security forces? If so, does the military provide leadership or support to that force, and to what extent? What percentage of the military is seconded to positions outside traditional military organizations?

What are the rules and procedures for triggering a military response to an internal security crisis? How do the military and other elements of the security system cooperate in such situations?

Who is responsible for border management in the country? Does the military play a major or supporting role?

Does the military perform police missions, and, if so, what are they and why?

Is the military involved in illicit activities, such as counternarcotics, and, if so, does it play a major or supporting role?

What is the role of the military in foreign and internal intelligence collection, and how does this role relate to those of the civilian intelligence services and the police? Have mechanisms been established for their cooperation and coordination?

Is the military involved in private sector activities, i.e., owning and running businesses, and, if so, what are they?

Is the military engaged in international peacekeeping operations, and, if so, are there positive and/or negative effects on the military overall?

Does the military have a role in providing social benefits, such as health or engineering services?

Is there corruption in the military, and, if so, is it widespread? What are the sources?

How politicized is the military in its leadership as well as among the rank and file, i.e., is the military (or particular groups within the military) linked to powerful political groups?

B. Composition of Military

What is the size of the military, and what services make up the military? Is the force designed, trained, and deployed to respond to the country's external and internal threats?

What is the rank structure in the different services? What is the salary structure in the different services? How do those salaries compare with jobs in the private sector?

Does the country have a conscript system? If so, what are the policies in terms of age and education?

What is the level of human capital (e.g., levels of literacy and education and prevalence of health conditions, such as HIV)?

Are there policies in place to ensure compliance with international legal obligations regarding child recruitment and child protection? What are they?

What is the ethnic and social composition of the military, and how representative is the military of society?

C. Military Organization

How is national command of the military structured in terms of command relationships and specific authorities? Is there a joint operational command?

Is there a general staff/joint staff/main staff? Is it organized to deal with issues at the military strategic level?

Do intelligence agencies fall under the general staff or under a civilian ministry?

D. Military Capabilities

What are the operational capabilities of the military overall and of each of the military services? Is the military able to operate throughout the country's territory? Is it able to support, sustain, and deploy forces outside its national borders?

What is the state of the military's equipment in each service? What types of mobility does the military have? Are ground, water, and air operations integrated?

Is the military interoperable with NATO and/or relevant regional or international forces (e.g., African Union, UN)?

Does the military have capabilities for the following:

- rapid reaction
- nighttime operations
- transport of personnel and naval amphibious operations
- satellite communication
- air interdiction operations, including maritime patrols
- integrated intelligence collection and analysis
- peacekeeping operations?

E. Military Readiness

What is the overall readiness of military personnel, including the following:

- How many military forces are on duty?
- How well are they trained?
- How many military forces are in reserve status?
- How well are they trained?

How robust is the military's command-and-control system? Is it being exercised? If not, would it be ready to be exercised if necessary?

What is the overall readiness of the military's logistics infrastructure?

How much equipment does the military have on hand and what are the equipment readiness rates?

What is the overall readiness of equipment in the military, including the following:

- vehicles
- radios
- weapons
- ammunition
- uniforms
- body armor
- helmets?

F. Military Logistics

Is there a logistics planning process/methodology? What are its characteristics?

Is there a process to manage the deployment of military forces, equipment, and cargo within the country? What are its characteristics? Is there a process to recover forces, equipment, and cargo? What are its characteristics?

Is there a process to manage the repair and maintenance of weapons, equipment, and vehicles? What are its characteristics?

Is adequate funding getting to units to conduct resupply and maintenance of equipment?

Does the military have accountability for supplies?

Is there a process to manage and administer fixed installations and locations that support the infrastructure for movement and transportation, supply, and accommodation inside the country as well as for deployments outside the country? What are its characteristics?

Is there a national logistics concept, and, if so, what functions does it include?

Has an inventory of critical infrastructure been prepared, and is there a plan to protect the critical logistics infrastructure?

G. Military Personnel Policies

Is there an established military recruitment system in place and functioning? What are its characteristics?

What accession standards are used for the selection of personnel (e.g., education, medical, age)? Do they differ for active and reserve forces? Do they differ for the different services?

What are the recruitment sources, policies, and incentives for officers, warrant officers, non-commissioned officers, and enlisted personnel?

Is there a process of promotion, career management, and dismissals to ensure that the best-qualified military personnel are retained? Is there evidence of "ghost soldiers" in the military?

How are former combatants integrated into the military?

Are military personnel regularly receiving their full paychecks?

What arrangements for pensions are in place for military personnel upon retirement or leaving the military?

Does the military have a social welfare system for its members?

Does the military have a professional military training and education system? What are its characteristics? Is there a policy document that describes it?

Is there training in international humanitarian law and human rights standards?

What is the attitude and response of the military toward HIV within its ranks? Is there consistently available counseling and testing? Is treatment available? What are the policies for HIV-positive soldiers?

H. Military Justice Policies

Is there a military justice system? Does it have a statutory basis? Are military personnel assigned and trained in military justice occupations?

Is the military justice system connected to the civilian justice system?

Does the military control areas of the country and impose military law?

Do pretrial facilities and prisons comprise a mixed civilian and military population? What role does the military have with regard to civilian prisons?

Does the military have jurisdiction over civilians?

Can a civilian law-enforcement officer arrest military service members?

Is the justice system applied equally to all members of the military?

What processes does the military have in place to respond to allegations of human rights violations by its personnel, including those relating to sexual and domestic violence?

Are there problems with corruption in the military justice system?

I. Military Doctrine

Is there a national military doctrine, a doctrine for each of the military services, or a joint military doctrine?

If there is a doctrine, is it based on a validated national security concept, national security strategy, and/or national military strategy?

Is there doctrine for how to work with other security agencies?

II. Conduct of Defense Policy

A. Role of Political Officials

What is the role of the president/prime minister in defense policymaking?

What ministries and agencies (e.g., foreign affairs, finance, justice) are involved in the conduct of defense policy, and have they been established in the constitution, law, policy, and/or regulation? Have these roles and missions been documented, clarified, and/or deconflicted?

Is there a role for officials in parliament in determining defense policy and expenditures? How is this accomplished (e.g., through a parliamentary commission or committee)? Does parliament have the authority and ability to carry out audits of defense expenditures? Does the parliament have adequate expertise in military matters to make informed decisions with respect to military policy and expenditures?

How transparent are military policy, spending, and management to parliamentarians, the media, and the general public?

What is the chain of command and division of responsibilities among political officials and military personnel? How does the actual exercise of control compare with the legal requirements?

What are the respective responsibilities of political officials and military leaders for the selection of senior military officers?

What mechanisms does the military have to raise legitimate concerns to its political leadership?

Are serving members of the military appointed to political positions within the government (e.g., ministerial positions, ambassadorships, directorships of nonmilitary organizations)?

Is there expertise among NGOs on military matters, and do NGOs participate in public discussion about military policy?

B. Ministry of Defense (MoD)

Organization

Is there a functioning MoD, and what is its size and organization?

Is the minister of defense a politically appointed civilian? What is the role of civilians in the ministry? What is the ratio of civilians to military personnel in the MoD? Is there an established civilian recruitment system in place and functioning? What are its characteristics?

How many civilian officials are recently retired military personnel?

What role does the MoD play in defense policy, strategic planning, financial management, weapon procurement, personnel recruitment, and logistics?

Responsibilities

Does the MoD have a strategic task list outlining its responsibilities and relationships to other organizations?

Does the MoD have the authority and processes to audit defense expenditures?

What are the roles of civilians and the military in defense strategy, planning, and budgeting? Are the respective responsibilities in the budgeting process clearly established in law, regulation, and procedures?

Does the MoD have a human resource policy and structure, and what are its characteristics?

C. Defense Strategy, Planning, and Budget

How are defense budgets prepared and implemented?

What budgeting methodology is used (e.g., zero-based budgeting or other)? What is the overall structure of defense budget (e.g., unit-based, activity-based, mixed)? For what time frame are financial resources preplanned or allocated (e.g., one year, two years, five years ahead)?

Is defense planning linked to programming and budgeting, and, if so, what techniques are used?

How are policy development, planning, programming, and management organized? Who is responsible for making decisions?

Is there a defense strategy? How is it formulated? What planning methodology is used (e.g., threat-based, resource-based, capability-based)?

Are there policy documents—long-term (e.g., national security strategy, white papers) and medium-term (e.g., national military strategy, national defense concept)—that influence funding decisions?

Are there financial management systems and procedures in place for accountability, anti-corruption, auditing, etc.? What are their characteristics? Are these procedures in law, directives, or regulations?

Does the military, branches of it, or local commanders control any revenue-generating operations, and, if so, which ones? Are all the incomes and expenditures from such operations part of the overall government budget?

What are the rules for procurement of major items of equipment, and how are these rules implemented?

Are there issues with corruption in the procurement process? What is being done to prevent and detect corruption?

III. Overall Political, Economic, and Security Environment

A. Political and Justice Systems

Does the government have a legal and security presence throughout the entire country, or are there ungoverned territories?

Does the government exercise control of the main lines of transportation, including rivers and roads? Is key infrastructure (e.g., energy) protected?

What type for political system does the country have, and what is the level of democratization in the country? Has there been a peaceful transfer of power from a ruling establishment to elected officials?

What are the characteristics and capacity of the country's criminal justice system? Have roles and missions among ministries and agencies been established in the constitution, law, policy, and regulations?

Does the justice system exist throughout the entire country? Are there alternative sources of justice outside the government?

What is the state of the judiciary? Are there sufficient judges, public defenders, investigators, prosecutors, and forensic experts? Is there evidence of bias in the decisions of the justice system?

How widespread is corruption, bribery, intimidation, and violence in the government and the justice sector? What mechanisms are in place to prevent, detect, and combat corruption?

Do security personnel receive human rights and international law training?

Does the justice system prosecute past human rights violators? Are human rights workers protected? Is there a witness protection program?

How are the law-enforcement agencies equipped?

Do law-enforcement agencies have adequate training and education to fulfill their missions?

Do the law-enforcement agencies have cooperative agreements or arrangements with regional or global law-enforcement organizations, such as INTERPOL?

Does the general populace see the law-enforcement agencies as protectors of the people or instruments of oppression?

B. Economic Situation

What is the state of the country's economic development? What type of economy does the country have, and what is the gross domestic product (GDP) per capita in the country? What percent of GDP is spent on the defense sector?

Is the government able to sustain military and civilian personnel, equipment, training, and operations without international financial assistance? If not, is there a plan for achieving financial sustainability? What are the government's potential sources of revenue collection?

What is the state of the country's physical infrastructure (e.g., electricity, roads, water)? How does this infrastructure affect the capabilities of the military?

C. Internal Conflicts

Are there internal conflicts? What are the current sources and status? Are there potential conflicts on the horizon?

What are the characteristics of these conflicts, including the social and ethnic components?

Who is involved in the conflicts (identify both governmental and nongovernmental groups and their social networks)?

Has there been a military role in the conflict, and has it changed over time?

Are nongovernmental security organizations (e.g., militias, paramilitaries) involved in the conflicts?

D. External Threats

Is there support from outside states for groups threatening the governments, e.g., terrorists, drug cartels, pirates?

What has been the role of the military in responding to these threats?

Assessment of Defense Institutions and Processes

This section involves an assessment of how the country's defense institutions and processes match up to what the United States views as the critical capacities of a defense sector. Based on the information collected in Section One, the assessment involves a qualitative appraisal of each of these capacities and then a quantitative scoring of each based on the following scale:

1. *Very Low:* entirely lacking
2. *Low:* beginning to develop
3. *Neither Low nor High:* Minimal but functioning
4. *High:* functional but room for improvement
5. *Very High:* strong and no major improvement needed.

Having outlined where deficiencies exist, the section poses another series of questions. The answers to these questions provide an overall assessment of the prospects in the country for improving its capacities in the areas in which deficiencies were found.

I. Assessment of Needs for Reform

Critical Capacities of the Defense Sector	Qualitative Assessment	Quantitative Assessment (Score 1 to 5)
Civilian control of military in practice, not just organization		
Systems of defense planning, procurement, budgeting, and financial management, including contracting and auditing		
Professionalism of military forces in terms of education and training		
Military personnel policies capable of recruiting, training, and retaining high-quality soldiers and officers representative of society as a whole		
Effective military command-and-control and logistics organizations		
Incorporation of rule of law and human rights components into military and MoD training programs		
Security forces carry out their functions in accordance with the principles of accountability, transparency, public participation, and respect for human rights		

II. Assessment of Prospects for Reform

The next step is to assess the prospects in the country for reforming the areas of deficiency identified in the first part of Section Two.

Has defense reform been undertaken in the past? Has it been part of an overall reform effort that includes the military, police, border guards, intelligence services, those government agencies that monitor such organizations, and those institutions charged with upholding the rule of law, including the judiciary and the penal system? Has defense sector reform been integrated within a larger state-building or democratization strategy? What have been the results? Are other countries or international organizations involved in reform efforts in the country?

Is the country's government willing to engage with the United States to reform the specific areas in which deficiencies were found?

Is the military willing to engage with the United States to reform the specific areas in which deficiencies were found? Are parts of the government supportive of reform and other parts opposed?

Are there groups outside the defense sector that are potentially supportive of (e.g., civil society groups) or opposed to (e.g., organized crime syndicates) such reforms?

Are there political, fiscal, or social constraints to such reforms?

What degree of public support is expected for such reforms?

Are other countries engaged in activities to reform the defense sector? What can be learned from their experiences?

Assessment of Counterterrorism and Counterinsurgency Capabilities

This section begins with a series of questions. The answers to these questions will provide an assessment of the country's overall counterterrorism and counterinsurgency capabilities. The section then involves a qualitative assessment of the country's capabilities to carry out the "critical" functions necessary to respond to a terrorism or insurgency threat. It then calls for a quantitative scoring of the country's capabilities based on the following scale:

1. *Very Low:* entirely lacking
2. *Low:* beginning to develop
3. *Neither Low nor High:* minimal but functioning
4. *High:* functional but room for improvement
5. *Very High:* strong and no major improvement needed.

Having outlined where deficiencies exist, the section poses another series of questions. The answers to these questions provide an overall assessment of the prospects in the country for improving its capabilities in the areas in which deficiencies were found.

I. Capabilities Assessment

Is the military involved in counterterrorism and counterinsurgency activities?

How well does the military operate with law-enforcement agencies in counterterrorism and/or counterinsurgency operations?

Are sufficient numbers of military forces involved in counterterrorism and counterinsurgency activities?

Does the military have planning, doctrine, and logistics support geared toward counterterrorism and counterinsurgency operations?

Are the military and police adequately trained in counterterrorism and counterinsurgency tactics?

Does the military have adequate equipment to conduct counterterrorism and/or counterinsurgency operations?

Does the government have the right type of information on terrorists or insurgents (e.g., what areas they are operating in, their prospects for expanding their operations, how they align themselves, their grievances)?

Does the government have an understanding of the support given to terrorists and insurgents by other states or international groups?

Is the military able to combat the tactics used by terrorists and insurgents from inside and outside the country?

Is the military able to process and share intelligence with other states effectively and quickly?

Does the government have sufficient ties to the domestic and international financial sector to disrupt terrorist financing?

Does the military include civil affairs units to conduct civil-military reconstruction/infrastructure projects aimed at winning over local civilians' support?

II. Assessment of Areas for Improvement in Capabilities

Critical Counterterrorism/ Counterinsurgency Functions	Qualitative Assessment	Quantitative Assessment (Score 1 to 5)
Maintain security throughout the country		
Collect and analyze intelligence		
Provide policing and law enforcement		
Protect critical infrastructure		
Carry out military surveillance and interdiction		
Integrate strategic communication		
Hold territory and control roadways, waterways, and airspace		
Contribute to the design and delivery of an overall integrated government strategy and operations		
Train military forces for counterterrorism or counterinsurgency operations		
Control corruption		
Disrupt financing by terrorist or insurgent groups from within or outside the country		
Deny support to terrorist or insurgent groups from domestic populations or from outside the country		

III. Assessment of Prospects for Improvement

The next step is to assess the prospects in the country for improving its capabilities in the areas of deficiency identified in the second part of Section Three.

Is the country's government willing to engage with the United States to improve its capabilities in the specific areas in which deficiencies were found?

Is the military willing to engage with the United States to improve its capabilities in the specific areas in which deficiencies were found?

Are there groups outside the defense sector that are potentially supportive of or opposed to such improvements?

Are there political, fiscal, or social constraints to such improvements?

What degree of public support is expected for such improvements?

Assessment of Counternarcotics Capabilities

This section begins with a series of questions. The answers to these questions provide an assessment of the country's overall counternarcotics capabilities. The section then involves a qualitative assessment of the country's capabilities to carry out the "critical" functions necessary to respond to the threat posed by drug trafficking. It then calls for a quantitative scoring of the country's capabilities based on the following scale:

1. *Very Low:* entirely lacking
2. *Low:* beginning to develop
3. *Neither Low nor High:* minimal but functioning
4. *High:* functional but room for improvement
5. *Very High:* strong and no major improvement needed.

Having outlined where deficiencies exist, the section then poses another series of questions. The answers to these questions provide an overall assessment of the prospects in the country for improving its capabilities in the areas in which deficiencies were found.

I. Capabilities Assessment

Is the military involved in counternarcotics activities?

Are there sufficient numbers of military forces to support the country's planned counternarcotics activities?

Does the military have planning, doctrine, and logistics support geared toward counternarcotics operations?

Are counternarcotics intelligence capabilities integrated across government agencies?

Does the military receive sufficient counternarcotics training? Does that include sufficient human rights and international law training?

Does the military have adequate counternarcotics equipment?

Is the size of the police force sufficient for counternarcotics operations, given the size and population of the country?

Does the police force have adequate equipment in the areas of communication and transportation?

Do the police receive sufficient training for counternarcotics operations?

Are police and military strategies and operations well integrated?

Does the government have the right type of information on the nature and dynamics of drug trafficking (e.g., what drugs are involved; what part of the production process is done in country; how the drugs are moved into, through, and out of the country; where traffickers operate; how heavily armed the traffickers are)?

Is the government able to adequately address crime and violence caused by drug trafficking?

Are there programs to demobilize and disarm those involved in the drug trade, and are these programs successful and sufficiently funded?

Are sufficient funds available for drug eradication, and does the public and military support these programs?

Are regional and bordering countries supportive of the counternarcotics efforts? Are any complicit in the drug trade?

Are there international donors (either other countries or international organizations) that are willing to contribute to the counternarcotics effort, and can they be expected to provide a long-term, sustained commitment?

Are there international efforts (e.g., air/coastal interdiction) to stop the import of unprocessed drugs or precursor elements?

II. Assessment of Areas for Improvement in Capabilities

Critical Counternarcotics Functions	Qualitative Assessment	Quantitative Assessment (Score 1 to 5)
Police, prosecute, and incarcerate drug traffickers		
Maintain law and order (public safety)		
Integrate military and law-enforcement operational support		
Maintain border and coastal security		
Collect intelligence on narcotics traffickers		
Control corruption		
Establish drug eradication and interdiction programs		
Develop rapid and mobile reaction capabilities based on real-time intelligence		
Train civilians and military forces in counternarcotics operations		
Control roadways, airspace, and waterways		

III. Assessment of Prospects for Improvement

The next step is to assess the prospects in the country for improving its capabilities in the areas of deficiency identified in the second part of Section Four.

Is the country's government willing to engage with the United States to improve its capabilities in the specific areas in which deficiencies were found?

Is the military willing to engage with the United States to improve its capabilities in the specific areas in which deficiencies were found?

Are there groups outside the defense sector that are potentially supportive of or opposed to such improvements?

Are there political, fiscal, or social constraints to such improvements?

What degree of public support is expected for such improvements?

Assessment of Border and Maritime Security Capabilities

This section begins with a series of questions. The answers to these questions provide an assessment of the country's overall border and maritime security capabilities. The section then involves a qualitative assessment of the country's capabilities to carry out the "critical" functions necessary to respond to a border or maritime security threat. It then calls for a quantitative scoring of the country's capabilities based on the following scale:

1. *Very Low:* entirely lacking
2. *Low:* beginning to develop
3. *Neither Low nor High:* minimal but functioning
4. *High:* functional but room for improvement
5. *Very High:* strong and no major improvement needed.

Having outlined where deficiencies exist, the section poses another series of questions. The answers to these questions provide an overall assessment of the prospects in the country for improving its capabilities in the areas in which deficiencies were found.

I. Capabilities Assessment

Who is responsible for border and maritime security? Are there sufficient numbers of military forces supporting such activities?

Do the army, coast guard, and navy have sufficient resources?

Are the army, coast guard, and navy able to respond adequately to incidents on the border, and are their interdiction capabilities adequate?

What is the relationship among the military, border police, and customs officials?

Does the military have the equipment it needs to conduct border and maritime security activities (e.g., small boats for maritime border security, helicopters for land border security, vehicles to patrol borders and ports)?

Does the military have effective onshore, offshore, and air intelligence, including surveillance, reconnaissance assets, and radar systems? Does it have adequate training and technical assistance with intelligence assets?

Is the military trained to conduct border and maritime security activities, or is additional training needed? Has the military received international training in border and maritime security activities?

Does the country have an effective computerized (automated) lookout/watch-list system for border control? Is it functional and being used?

Is there effective coordination between government institutions that conduct border and maritime security activities?

Do government institutions share information and intelligence?

Is there sufficient coordination between independent international or regional border and maritime security activities?

Does the international community provide support to the country to improve border and maritime security?

II. Assessment of Areas for Improvement in Capabilities

Critical Border and Maritime Security Functions	Qualitative Assessment	Quantitative Assessment (Score 1 to 5)
Patrol and secure land and marine borders		
Track people and goods entering and leaving the country		
Control corruption		
Coordinate with neighboring states and international community on border security		
Collect intelligence and conduct border surveillance		
Train military forces on border and maritime security while border security tasks are transitioned to nonmilitary border management agency		

III. Assessment of Prospects for Improvement

The next step is to assess the prospects in the country for improving its capabilities in the areas of deficiency indentified in the second part of Section Five.

Is the country's government willing to engage with the United States to improve its capabilities in the specific areas in which deficiencies were found?

Is the military willing to engage with the United States to improve its capabilities in the specific areas in which deficiencies were found?

Are there groups outside the defense sector that are potentially supportive of or opposed to such improvements?

Are there political, fiscal, or social constraints to such improvements?

What degree of public support is expected for such improvements?

Assessment of Counterpiracy Capabilities

This section begins with a series of questions. The answers to these questions provide an assessment of the country's overall counterpiracy capabilities. The section then involves a qualitative assessment of the country's capabilities to carry out the "critical" functions necessary to respond to a piracy threat. It then calls for a quantitative scoring of the country's capabilities based on the following scale:

1. *Very Low:* entirely lacking
2. *Low:* beginning to develop
3. *Neither Low nor High:* minimal but functioning
4. *High:* functional but room for improvement
5. *Very High:* strong and no major improvement needed.

Having outlined where deficiencies exist, the section poses another series of questions. The answers to these questions provide an overall assessment of the prospects in the country for improving its capabilities in those areas in which deficiencies were found.

I. Capabilities Assessment

Does the military have adequate staff, boats, equipment, and training to successfully conduct counterpiracy operations?

Does it have an adequate command-and-control center for counterpiracy?

Does the military or a civilian organization have screening protocols and systems aimed at identifying arriving and departing vessels, the crews that staff the ships, and/or the companies that own and run them?

Does the military have capabilities to respond to incidents at sea: interdict and board suspected pirate vessels, intervene against attacks in progress, communicate after ships have been seized, and retake ships?

Does the country have what it needs in terms of onshore, offshore, and air intelligence, including surveillance, reconnaissance assets, and radar systems? Do military and civilian organizations have adequate training and technical assistance with intelligence assets?

Does the government have adequate knowledge about the pirates (e.g. motivation, age, income, ethnicity/religion, education level)?

Does the government have the ability to gather, assess, and share intelligence on pirate financial operations, including information about onshore investors? Is the government able to track and freeze ransoms?

Is the government undertaking activities to dismantle active safe havens that the pirates occupy on land?

Is the government able to stop the flow of weapons, equipment, and funds to the pirates?

Is the government combating other illegal maritime activities, such as illegal fishing, drug smuggling, or trafficking in arms and persons?

Are other security priorities diverting potential resources and equipment away from counterpiracy operations?

Are there mechanisms in place for military coordination with the justice sector for prosecution, including collection of evidence, information sharing, transfer of custody, potential extradition to another country, etc.?

Does the country have the requisite legal foundation aside from customary international law and universal jurisdiction over piracy to investigate and prosecute such cases?

II. Assessment of Areas for Improvement in Capabilities

Critical Counterpiracy Functions	Qualitative Assessment	Quantitative Assessment (Score 1 to 5)
Patrol shorelines and waterways		
Respond to incidents at sea, including boarding and retaking pirated vessels		
Collect and analyze intelligence on pirate financing		
Conduct surveillance and reconnaissance of ships at sea		
Identify vessels arriving and departing from territorial waters		
Disrupt and dismantle pirate bases ashore		
Prosecute and incarcerate pirates		
Communicate with private vessels, international security forces, and own military forces		
Coordinate with regional and international military forces		
Conduct counterpiracy training and exercises		

III. Assessment of Prospects for Improvement

The next step is to assess the prospects in the country for improving its capabilities in the areas of deficiency identified in the second part of Section Six.

Is the country's government willing to engage with the United States to improve its capabilities in the specific areas in which deficiencies were found?

Is the military willing to engage with the United States to improve its capabilities in the specific areas in which deficiencies were found?

Are there groups outside the defense sector that are potentially supportive of or opposed to such improvements?

Are there political, fiscal, or social constraints to such improvements?

What degree of public support is expected for such improvements?

Assessment of Capabilities to Stabilize Postconflict Situations

This section begins with a series of questions. The answers to these questions provide an assessment of the country's overall capabilities to stabilize postconflict situations. The section then involves a qualitative assessment of the country's capabilities to carry out the "critical" functions necessary to respond to the instability arising from postconflict situations. It then calls for a quantitative scoring of the country's capabilities based on the following scale:

1. *Very Low:* entirely lacking
2. *Low:* beginning to develop
3. *Neither Low nor High:* minimal but functioning
4. *High:* functional but room for improvement
5. *Very High:* strong and no major improvement needed.

Having determined where deficiencies exist, the section then poses another series of questions. The answers to these questions provide an overall assessment of the prospects in the country for improving its capabilities in the areas in which deficiencies were found.

I. Capabilities Assessment

Has there been a clear resolution of the conflict, through a peace treaty, peace process, or political reconciliation?

Have the military forces involved in the prior conflict been disbanded, disarmed, and/or merged into existing military? Are there personnel records or statistics on these individuals, such as education, medical history, and criminal records, to assist the process?

Have there been successful efforts to stem the illegal and legal proliferation of weapons, such as weapon buyback programs or new gun laws?

If the military is responsible for demilitarization activities, does it have the capabilities to destroy the munitions? If not, what additional capabilities are needed?

Are there sufficient programs and funds to reintegrate the military into civil society, including through education or employment?

Are there adequate processes in place to deal with those who committed human rights abuses during the conflict, such as transitional justice systems or the prosecution of war crimes?

Are there adequate programs for soldiers wounded in action or for families of those killed in action?

Are there sufficient efforts to deal with ethnic/religious issues in the security sector, such as ensuring geographic and ethnic inclusiveness in the military and police?

Has the government been successful in reducing the role of alternative sources of insecurity, including paramilitaries, private armies, local civil defense forces, guerilla forces, or warlords?

If private military contractors are providing security, have there been efforts to address potentially problematic contractual issues with the U.S. government or issues related to secrecy?

Are adequate systems in place to address the issue of displaced persons and refugees?

Are there programs to rebuild basic infrastructure destroyed during the conflict?

Are there sufficient efforts to combat sources of instability, including regional threats, organized crime, violent street crime, smuggling (drugs and otherwise), human trafficking, and youth unemployment?

II. Assessment of Areas for Improvement in Capabilities

Critical Postconflict Stabilization Functions	Qualitative Assessment	Quantitative Assessment (Score 1 to 5)
Maintain internal peace and security		
Ensure rule of law through effective judicial system		
Defend against international threats		
Restore or provide basic government services		
Repair critical infrastructure		
Introduce civilian control of the military		
Demobilize, disarm, and reintegrate former soldiers		
Control the proliferation of weapons		
Train and recruit new military and police forces		

III. Assessment of Prospects for Improvement

The next step is to assess the prospects in the country for improving its capabilities in the areas of deficiency identified in the second part of Section Seven.

Is the country's government willing to engage with the United States to improve its capabilities in the specific areas in which deficiencies were found?

Is the military willing to engage with the United States to improve its capabilities in the specific areas in which deficiencies were found?

Are there groups outside the defense sector that are potentially supportive of or opposed to such improvements?

Are there political, fiscal, or social constraints to such improvements?

What degree of public support is expected for such improvements?

What can be expected in terms of public support for such improvements?